more

more

FIND YOUR PERSONAL CALLING
AND LIVE LIFE TO
THE FULLEST MEASURE

TODD WILSON

FOREWORD BY RICK WARREN AND ROBERT COLEMAN

ZONDERVAN

More
Copyright © 2016 by Todd Wilson

This title is also available as a Zondervan ebook.
Visit www.zondervan.com/ebooks.

This title is also available as a Zondervan audio book.
Visit www.zondervan.com/fm.

Requests for information should be addressed to:
Zondervan, 3900 *Sparks Dr. SE, Grand Rapids, Michigan* 49546

Library of Congress Cataloging-in-Publication Data

    Names: Wilson, Todd A., 1976- author.
    Title: More : find your personal calling and live life to the fullest measure
      / by Todd Wilson.
    Description: Grand Rapids : Zondervan, 2016.
    Identifiers: LCCN 2015040685 | ISBN 9780310524250 (softcover)
    Subjects: LCSH: Vocation—Christianity.
    Classification: LCC BV4740 .W495 2016 | DDC 248.4—dc23 LC record available at
      http://lccn.loc.gov/2015040685

Published in association with the literary agency of Mark Sweeney & Associates, Bonita
Springs, Florida 34135.

Cover design: Brand Navigation
Cover image: 123RF.com
Interior design: Denise Froehlich

Printed in the United States of America

16 17 18 19 20 21 22 23 /DHV/ 15 14 13 12 11 10 9 8 7 6 5 4 3 2 1

To Jesus,
who makes it possible for us to take hold of exceedingly,
abundantly more in this life

To Anna,
my wonderful bride and partner for over three decades,
who has faithfully stood by my side,
encouraging most every step,
and filling the voids created by my weaknesses

Contents

Foreword

BY PASTOR RICK WARREN AND
DR. ROBERT COLEMAN

More is one of those unique books coming at just the right time, with just the right message, and written to everyday folks. You will be inspired and convicted to action. You will see your personal calling in a new light.

Jesus said, "I am come that they might have life, and that they might have it more abundantly" (John 10:10 KJV). Some translations of Jesus' words use "life to the full" or "to the fullest measure." Unfortunately, too many people pursue abundance in all the wrong ways, year after year, only to find emptiness.

What would happen in our generation if Christians were to rise up and show the world what it looks like to have the fullness of Jesus in them? What would it look like for that fullness to overflow into the world as love in action? What if we were to truly embrace the truth that God's unique personal calling is his gift for equipping us to play our part in his mission in the world?

I [Rick Warren] have walked with Todd Wilson and been part of his team at Exponential for several years. He cares deeply about Jesus and the church. He is a student and lifelong learner. His passion for living for God's glory and helping others do the same is genuine. I'm proud of how he has used the gifts God gave him, and I encourage you to learn from his experience.

In *More*, my friend Todd provides a fresh framework for helping others discover and engage their personal calling. With the creativity of an artist, the insights of an engineer, and the experience of a lifetime learner, Todd explains the idea of God's personal calling for each of our lives.

Todd reminds us that while each of us has a unique calling, we also share a common calling that unites us in a common mission. Specifically, we are all called to be disciples of Jesus who make disciples. We are called to BE like Christ, DO good works, and GO wherever he sends us.

More challenges us to fulfill God's calling instead of pursuing our own personal fulfillment. It is only in giving our lives away that we find the meaning of our lives. Significance does not come from sex or salary or status. It comes from serving. Todd is a great example of someone who has made the transition from simply pursuing a career to fulfilling a calling.

I [Robert Coleman] am honored to have played a part in Todd's journey and the writing of *More*. When you spend time with Todd, you can't help but see his passion for the kingdom of God and his heart for multiplication. He is a strategic futurist who naturally sees and understands the importance and power of a fully devoted follower of Jesus released on mission.

Todd is giving his life to modeling what it looks like to live in your unique sweet spot of personal calling and to equip others to do the same. He is not a theorist with good ideas. Instead he is a practitioner with lots of experience in the trenches.

Many books have been written on discipleship. Many books have also been written on calling. *More* finds the unique intersection of both. Using the lens of discipleship, *More* brings the truth of personal calling to life, and this brings joy to my soul. I'm encouraged by the impact this book will have in advancing the conversation about discipleship and in mobilizing the latent capacity of calling to action within the body of Christ.

We don't have to reinvent Jesus' ways. We simply need to rediscover them and put them into practice. That is exactly what Todd helps us do with the idea of personal calling.

Jesus started his movement in the most humble and nonconventional of ways. He didn't start with a tagline, a clever business model, political clout, or a massive platform of influence. He started with ordinary people called to extraordinary things. He started with disciples called to make disciples wherever they were.

The ripple of that common calling extends to us today. He's still calling all of us to be his hands and his feet. He's still calling us to be his voice.

Our prayer is that you'll read these words and find your deepest purpose in life. That as ordinary folks we will once again rise up to simply become disciples. And in that title we'll find everything God has created us to be.

God is calling. And when you answer, this world will never be the same.

Introduction: There Must Be Something More

I have come so that they may have life, and have it to the full.

JOHN 10:10

There has to be more." These words echoed in his ears with ever-increasing intensity, invading his daily routine to the depths of his soul. In years past he could escape it for days at a time, sometimes even weeks or months. But not anymore. It was there. Always there. Always lurking. Always stirring and never quite satisfied.

Eat. Sleep. Work. Conquer. Repeat. His heart felt like it was stuck. He found himself questioning how his environment— his friends, his community, his circumstances, and even his work—might be the cause of his discontentment. And yet this feeling seemed to emanate from deep inside his soul, so deep that it couldn't possibly be caused by anything external. It was a seed planted when God had knit him together in his mother's womb. It was a seed longing to sprout and blossom into fruit.

His family was fine; his business was going well. There were issues, but that was normal. He was successful and admired, living the life he'd dreamed of as a young man, and yet he felt unfulfilled. He was successful and comfortable, yet seemingly so insignificant and unsatisfied. The questions lingered.

Is this all there is? What is my purpose? What should I
be doing to have the biggest impact? There were as many
questions as there were days. The longing for something
more was growing more intense. He was a driven man,
always able to tackle a problem and conquer the next hill. But
this one was getting the best of him. It was so elusive.

He felt ordinary and extraordinary at the same time. He
knew and trusted God but often wondered why his Creator
felt so distant and disengaged from the details of his life. Did
he need to be more proactive, or should he wait patiently?
He did not want to get ahead of God and force things, but the
waiting was one degree short of agonizing. He felt so stuck
and powerless.

Like gold hidden in a mattress, he felt deeply the weight
of unused potential. He wondered if he would ever engage the
mission God designed for him. Would he ever have the unique
impact he was made for? Those questions haunted him.

It was a morning like any other, with the same old
routine. He settled into the rhythm of household chores,
breakfast, and his walk to the job site. He sighed at the
thought of the same old results and another restless day.
Then it happened. He really wasn't expecting it, but somehow
he'd never been more ready. The time had come, and the seed
was ready to burst forth into the light of day. The "yes" was
as good as spoken before the question was even asked.

The man was Peter, and the catalyzing event was Jesus'
call. As Jesus walked beside the shoreline, his words to Peter,
a simple fisherman, were simple and powerful. "Come, follow
me!" (Matthew 4:19). No verbal response was required. "At
once [Peter] left [his] nets and followed him" (Matthew 4:20).
Peter acted immediately, giving his heart, his head, and his
hands fully to Jesus. He stepped into the Master's service
with no conditions and no reservations.

There Has to Be More

Do you ever feel like Peter must have felt before he responded
to the call of Christ? The same Peter who was a fisherman

living in the obscurity of a small rural village. He was a man struggling day by day to provide for his family and make the best of this life, a man who spent the first half of his life unaware that so much *more* was in store.

We know Peter's impact downstream of that profound "yes," but we often forget the years of struggle he may have experienced to prepare him for that day. The story behind the story (or before the story) is always critical. The journey leading up to our "yes" positions us for the surrender that ultimately produces a future of more: more fullness, more abundance, and more contentment.

The discontent we feel, the deep conviction that there must be something more, the yearning to live faithfully in God's calling, these are all seeds planted and watered by God.

Profound questions have been asked by every generation and will continue to be the heart of our most important searching. First, what does it mean to be human? Who are we at a fundamental level? Second, what should we do? What does virtue look like in the realm of action? Third, where is our context, or the position of our best selves? What is the perfect environment to fully release our potential?

More provides a framework to tackle these questions head on. It starts with who we are, and that we are uniquely created with a unique identity and design. Who are we created to BE? This identity is one we actively discover and participate in activating. Our BE or identity overflows into and shapes our mission. What are we made to DO? Finally, our DO requires a context, or a position where it is lived out. Where are we to GO?

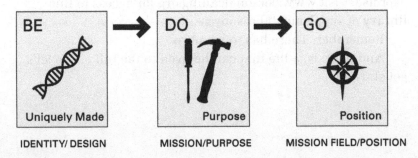

IDENTITY/ DESIGN   MISSION/PURPOSE   MISSION FIELD/POSITION

More is full of insights and tools for working through these BE-DO-GO elements. All of these working together lead to the fullness of God's call on our lives.

This project is a celebration of the idea that there is *more* and that God wants us to experience it. My prayer is that this book will refresh and challenge your thinking regarding personal calling and give you a means for discovering and engaging God's calling on your life. The BE-DO-GO framework seeks to provide a simple vocabulary and lens to pursue your unique personal calling.

Strategies and plans are important, but don't miss the often overlooked truth that Jesus changed the world with twelve leaders who surrendered themselves with a "yes" and then embarked on a journey of discovering and engaging their personal calling.

Twelve ordinary men with convictions to live out their destiny started the greatest movement in the history of the world. They became leaders who allowed the seed God planted in their souls to sprout, grow, and produce incredible fruit. God desires the same for you, but you have a decision to make. Will you commit to discover your unique calling and engage it as faithfully as you can?

The first section of this book highlights ten truths of personal calling and provides a framework for understanding and discovering one's personal calling. The second section provides a roadmap for applying the framework. Discovering your calling is a process that takes time and reflection. I've developed a library of tools to assist you in completing the exercise. Visit www.personalcalling.org for access to this library of supplemental resources.

Remember: There has to be more.

And there is, a life that can be lived to the full . . . so let's get started!

PART ONE

Foundations in Calling

CHAPTER 1

Trusting the Author of Our Story

Let us run with perseverance the race that is
set before us, fixing our eyes on Jesus, the pioneer
and perfecter of faith.

HEBREWS 12:1B–2A

I love visiting a friend's historic farm where I take friends to facilitate one-on-one sessions on personal calling. For even the most history-impaired learners, this place is inescapably inspirational. From the living quarters dating to the 1760s, to the bricks that previously served as ballast weights in trade ships from England, this sprawling estate spans the annals of our entire history as a nation. To visit is to see, smell, and feel the presence of our founding fathers. Quite literally.

I start every session with a short walk to the oldest and largest oak tree I've ever seen. In fact, it dates to nearly the time that a young man named George Washington visited the property as a teenager to survey the land for its owner, Lord Fairfax. Although Washington's family did well financially, their Mount Vernon estate passed mostly to George's older brother. Washington found himself looking for his first full-time vocational job.

As good fortune would have it, he had connections with the wealthy Fairfax family, who owned nearly 5.3 million acres of land in Virginia. To protect his property rights, Lord Fairfax needed trusted land surveyors. In those days, a good surveyor could make as much money as a trial lawyer, and the networking connections were unparalleled. Lord Fairfax was impressed with the young, energetic, and talented Washington and hired him to help with surveying.

I start the facilitation standing by that giant oak tree with the question, "What was George Washington thinking as a seventeen-year-old kid when he was here in 1749 surveying this property? He had his entire life ahead of him, with so many dreams and so many possibilities. So what was he thinking?"

Let's start with what he was not thinking. There was no United States, and hence he could have no aspirations of being president. There were not yet any revolutionaries, and hence no need for a commanding general or army. There was no family inheritance so no Mount Vernon estate to run. In fact, all Washington had was the dreams and hopes of a prosperous future. So landing a lucrative position as a surveyor for Fairfax was a very strategic and promising launch pad for his future. In some ways, a dream job for Washington. But not in the way he expected!

In reading George Washington's journal from those early surveying days, we see that he had plenty of time on his hands. Time to think. Time to wrestle with life's most important questions. Time to ponder the same kinds of questions we wrestle with today, like "What is the purpose for my life?"

The plans ordained for young Washington were impossible for him to comprehend, let alone dream up. Washington's thoughts at seventeen most certainly focused on dreams of things not yet formed, but that were possible to see and comprehend. Dreams that would take hard work, an industrious attitude, and strong leadership. Yet dreams that were not the core story yet to be written in Washington's life.

How often is this true in our lives? We desperately want clarity today. The paradigm shaping our future story is that which we know and that which we can dream and see in color today. We want the heroic, adventurous, and impactful life that Washington had, but we become convinced that stories like his are only experienced by a select few people.

The problem isn't that we want too much—it's that we want too little. Instead of experiencing an adventurous journey with God and gaining an ever-increasing clarity on who he made us to be, we become stuck in today. We fail to embrace and step into the story God has uniquely designed for us.

A Bigger Narrative

What if our bigger narrative is a journey to be pursued? A story to be more fully developed and written? Isn't that the story of the heroes of our faith?

Think of Peter's early days. Did he have any idea he would one day found and lead the early church? Even as he lived with Jesus and ministered with him, did he have any idea that he would be a household name thousands of years later? That his words and letters would become Scripture?

How about Abraham? We see him as larger than life—a seven-foot-tall glowing titan who spoke with God directly—a figure of legend. But did Abraham realize the breadth of God's work to create a nation, and how that nation would pave the way for Messiah to come to earth? Did he know how much of a mark on the earth he would leave as he obeyed God's call to "Go"?

How about Ruth, who faithfully served her mother-in-law Naomi after the death of their husbands? She left her homeland in Moab and followed Naomi to a foreign country. Did she know she would become the ancestor of King David and eventually Jesus?

These were great men and women of God, heroes of the faith, used in amazing and miraculous ways to accomplish

God's purpose on the earth. What if they had chosen a different path? Do you think they would have experienced the discontent we know too well? Do you think their heart of hearts would have been troubled?

What about us? Do we have a sense of how critical our path might be to future generations? That our story will impact an entire generation of leaders in ways we simply cannot see today? The foundational idea we must begin with is to accept the truth that God has created us and has created our context, putting those two things together with a good result in mind.

No Blueprints for the Manuscript

How often does God laugh in response to one of the most frequent prayers he hears, "God show me, and I will follow"? He knows that showing us the full picture all at once is the worst thing he can do. He wants our obedience today in small steps based on what he does reveal. He calls us to be faithful with little, so that he can entrust us with much.

Remember those early years Washington spent as a surveyor traveling through the land that would eventually host the Revolutionary War. If you could select a leader to command the Revolutionary forces, what better qualifications could you ask for than that of surveyor of the land where the battles would be fought? A surveyor who knows the land, its contours, its rivers, and its valleys, and who has relationships with many of its inhabitants.

George Washington's time as a surveyor was preparing him for something much bigger than he understood at the time. But if Washington had allowed surveying to be his final destination, he would have missed the greater purposes ordained for him.

We may no longer be seventeen, with our whole lives in front of us. Most likely we have already made choices and started on our life's journey. Our first responsibility is to wake up to the higher purpose of what God may be doing with our life and then to be a good steward of what God gives us to work with right now. Life itself is our laboratory for discovering and learning more about what God wants us to do, about the story he is writing with our lives. God's command to Abram to "Go" enabled him to discover his true calling as the father of many nations. Jesus' call to Peter to "follow me" led to three years of experiential learning, where Peter learned to "feed my sheep" (John 21:17), ultimately founding and building the church we know today.

Like most great adventures, the journey is not proscriptive or directive. Os Guinness, author of *The Call*, makes a distinction between guidance and calling. He says, "'Guidance' and 'calling' certainly overlap, but guidance is generally specific. God tells us to 'do this,' 'go there,' 'don't do this,' 'don't go there'—through the Bible and the Holy Spirit. But calling is generally entrepreneurial. In most areas of life we do not hear God's voice or see any vision from God. Like the servants in the parable of the talents, we go about the Master's business, seeking to multiply and maximize the talents he has entrusted to us."[1]

The story God is writing in us isn't something that we passively receive. The mystery is that God wants us to participate in this story in an active way. As we search out God's calling on our life, we can discover a depth of truth and a level of freedom that may have previously seemed elusive. God desires to write our story in a way that leads to greatness of heart. As we respond to his call, life becomes an adventure, and we will feel a sense of deep satisfaction and joy, even in the midst of difficulty and suffering.

Making It Personal

To live out my calling, I must first believe that God has a calling and purpose for my life, and that I need to actively engage in finding and developing that calling.

trusting
the Author of Our Story

Calling is discovered when we believe that our lives are a story written by God.

Calling moves us from seeing life as random to embracing God's handiwork in the events of life. Every experience, both good and bad, reveals more of his will and plan for our lives. Finding our calling requires trust in the author of our story.

Calling Foundations

Clarity of calling emerges when we learn to:

1. Trust deeply the author of our story.

Visit www.personalcalling.org for supplemental resources.

CHAPTER 2

Stepping Forward in Faith

When he had spit on the man's eyes and
put his hands on him, Jesus asked, "Do you see
anything?"

He looked up and said, "I see people; they
look like trees walking around." Once more Jesus
put his hands on the man's eyes. Then his eyes
were opened, his sight was restored, and he saw
everything clearly.

MARK 8:23B–25

The Grand Tetons are beautiful, so I'm told. They are
a subrange of the Rocky Mountains in Wyoming and
contain some of the most photographed landscapes in the
world. They rise majestically, blending earth and sky in a way
that few places on earth can rival. I was looking forward to
seeing them.

We had scheduled a gathering of close friends at a house
near these mountains for rest, reflection, and catching up
with one another. For months the anticipation grew with
friends saying, "You won't believe the view!" The entire front
of the house was made of giant windows to accentuate and
appreciate the panoramic view of one of the best landscapes
known to man. The trip was scheduled and it was finally

happening. I was going to see this great vista with my own eyes.

A couple of days before the flight, I was told to be sure and get a window seat. So I did, wangling a spot in line and capturing a window seat in visual expectation.

As we landed at 10:30 p.m., the landscape was breathtakingly, well, dark. I couldn't see anything—it was nighttime. The great scenery covered in darkness was amusing, but not to worry, tomorrow morning we'd awake to the beautiful Grand Tetons.

I rose early and walked to the sea of glass, more than ready to experience the magnificent . . . fog. Fog in all its fogginess, with no mountains to be seen. The Grand Fog was not inspiring at all. Again, amidst the laughter, friends told me not to worry—the fog always burned off by early afternoon, and the wonderful landscape would make a glorious appearance.

Nope. The fog didn't burn off. I never experienced the long-awaited grand view. To this day, in spite of the proximity of the range, I've still not seen the Grand Tetons.

Here's the thing. As a result of my visit, should I conclude the mountains are not there or that they are not beautiful? Of course not.

Also, all was not lost. Far from it. God used those days and that experience to get my attention and to speak to me in a way that the unobstructed, beautiful, clear landscape never could have.

On the plane ride home, I wrote down two reflections. First, the clarity I have (or don't have) does not change the beauty and sovereignty of what is hidden behind the fog. I need to move forward trusting that the clarity will come and acting as if it already did.

Second, I realized that theoretically you can drive across the country in fog, never seeing more than ten feet in front of you. To be sure, that kind of journey is slow, draining, and difficult as you strain to see the road, but you can still get there. The journey is not always easy in the fog, but we can make progress.

Redefining Clarity

As we consider the idea of clarity, we need a slight redefinition of the term. We normally think of clarity in terms of eyesight and understanding. If we have a journey on a clear day, with an unobstructed view, we can make better progress. But clarity as it relates to decisions and progress is as related to *trust* as it is to understanding and seeing clearly.

Sometimes the fog is on the window inside the car. This is one we can do something about. Set the defrost! Grab a cloth and wipe the condensation off of the window! Understanding that sometimes we can improve our own clarity is a useful realization. We should do all we can in this regard.

Now consider the blind man with a seeing-eye dog. He doesn't see at all but trusts the signals of his canine guide to let him step forward safely. Sometimes the clarity we experience allowing us to move forward is based on trust and limited input, instead of crystal-clear vision. The car traveling through fog can't simply wipe it away. Instead, the driver must use what sight he has to cautiously and deliberately move forward.

We must learn to distinguish between "God fog" and "self fog." Sometimes God allows fog into our lives as part of his purposes, to teach us increased trust and patience or to protect us from moving too quickly. There are other times when the lack of clarity is on our end—"self fog"—and there are things we are doing (or not doing) that actually prolong or even worsen the fog.

I couldn't do anything to see the Grand Tetons. The darkness and fog were beyond my control, but every bit of beauty was there to be discovered on another day. I could have dwelt on the fog and missed what God was trying to teach me.

The more quickly we embrace the truth that God cares more about our blind steps of faith and surrender than he does about our clarity and comfort, the sooner we will be positioned to more fully understand the story God has written in our lives.

The Promise: A Masterpiece to Be Discovered

Each of us, individually, is a masterpiece. Most of us don't see ourselves that way, but according to Ephesians 2:10, it is literally true: you are a masterpiece conceived by God before the beginning of the world and placed perfectly in creation to accomplish a purpose that he has planned. Once we grasp this idea at a heart level, it changes our perspective and attitude. It also changes our persistence.

Imagine that someone gives you the following job: See if you can find a needle in that stack of hay. Some people would laugh at the request and not even try. Others might look through the hay but give up quickly because the assignment subtly implies there may not be a needle. Most people would return and report that they checked the haystack but could not find the needle.

Now imagine we frame the task differently: There is a needle in that pile of hay. Your job is to find it. Don't come back until you do. There's a reward for you when you find it!

Would you search differently if you knew with certainty the needle was there and could be found? You might break the haystack down into manageable sections and search each smaller pile thoroughly before moving on to the next. You might get other people involved. You would look until you found it and would come back successful, needle in hand.

The difference between finding the needle and not finding it starts in the mind.

In a similar way, the pursuit of calling starts in the mind. Do you really believe that God has uniquely gifted you and is writing an important story in your life? What you believe about God's promise (that we are a masterpiece created as the workmanship of his hands, and that he designed good works and a purpose for us before we were born) creates a lighthouse that no fog can suppress.

Starting with What We Have

Imagine you're putting together a thousand-piece puzzle of the Grand Tetons, but the photo on the box is a digital image that changes each day. Each time you sit down to assemble pieces, you see a different perspective, only one small part of the picture, or worse yet, fog. So goes our journey. We tend to become paralyzed when all we see is fog.

Our step of faith is to move forward on our journey in the absence of a clear road map and picture of the destination.

How do we make progress when all we see is fog? Find the corner pieces—and we know where those go. No picture required. Find the edge pieces, and with a little time and work we are able to outline a frame for our mountainous view. No picture required. As we do, we discover that the pieces we've put in place solidify a living picture that is even better than the printed picture on a box. Momentum builds as pieces are put in place and clarity emerges.

We simply start with what we have and what we know to be true. We build on that foundation, little by little, bit by bit, till a picture begins to take shape.

Click—Click. Better or Worse?

The sense of who we are and what God is leading us to do comes into focus slowly as we pursue the idea of his calling. Consider our physical eyesight as an example:

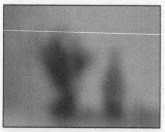

This is an image similar to the perception and focus of 20:800 vision. It's very blurry. There are two or three basic shapes, but the detail is elusive. It might be an arrangement of flowers and a bottle.

Now consider the image again, this time at 20:400. That still isn't good, but it's much better. We can discern a vase of flowers, a bottle, and a couple of other objects on the table. The object on the right could be just about anything. The picture is better, but we still aren't in focus.

Click-click. Let's make a bigger jump and go to 20:80 vision: That's better, isn't it? We begin to see definition in the flowers and bottle now, though the blurry objects in the middle are still unclear, but the object on the right is a piece of fruit.

Let's come into focus and see what we have: 20:20 vision is a beautiful thing, isn't it? A pitcher of flowers, branches, walnuts, a bottle, and an apple . . . all emerging from the lack of clarity that we first experienced.

One thing that makes the journey to our calling difficult is that our clarity is often much closer to 20:800 than 20:20. We often won't be able to take a solid step into a sharper picture until we engage. Things get clearer as we go.

Imagine for a moment that you're an eye doctor and George Washington is in the chair, getting fitted for a prescription in his life's calling. You're looking over the picture of his entire life, related to his calling and purpose, looking for the perfect lens to see most clearly. You're adjusting the lens and asking Washington if his vision for the course of his life is better or worse.

Click-click: Your father dies when you are eleven and the inheritance goes to your brother. Better or worse?

Click-click: Your mother wants you to have a commission in the Royal Navy, but that does not work out. Better or worse?

Click-click: You become good friends with George William Fairfax, cousin of Lord Fairfax. Better or worse?

Click-click: Your brother is head of the Virginia militia. When he dies, you assume that role. Better or worse?

Click-click: You are continually affirmed for your strategic military mind, your leadership skills, and your ability to get things done. Better or worse?

Click-click: You become a successful business leader with a natural affinity for hard work and making the most of opportunity. Better or worse?

Click-click: You are naturally drawn to politics and its influence. Better or worse?

You can see the patterns that emerge in Washington's story, even from a young age. His journey, even the apparent setbacks and failures, produced more clarity over time, just as ours does. Finding his calling was a lifelong process with him becoming president in his final decade of life.

The picture beyond the fog is beautiful. It's worth it. Remember to trust and keep moving forward as you embrace the fog that covers the beautiful landscape of your calling.

Be diligent and trust the author; move forward and step into his story, even if your vision is not yet clear. Your longing for more starts and ends with him!

Making It Personal

To embrace the truths of calling I will step forward in faith, trusting deeply that God, the author of my story, has written a unique script for me.

stepping
Forward in Faith

Calling is discovered in trusting we are a masterpiece, uniquely created for fullness and good works, when this is hard to see.

Calling moves us from being paralyzed in our perceived insignificance to finding profound significance in our unique design, not because of what we do but because of who created us. Because of trust, we can embrace the fog, taking steps of faith and trust beyond what we can clearly see. As we do, we will learn which fog is self-inflicted and which is provided by God to protect us. This moves us from needing perfect clarity to instead living in loving trust of our heavenly Father.

Calling Foundations

Clarity of calling emerges when we learn to:

1. Trust deeply the author of our story.
2. Step forward in faith, even when we cannot see clearly.

Visit www.personalcalling.org for supplemental resources.

CHAPTER 3

Two Scripts, Two Kingdoms

What is your life? You are a mist that appears
for a little while and then vanishes.

JAMES 4:14

Samantha was our obedient Labrador retriever given to
us as a wedding present. She had a strong pedigree from
a championship line and had to be the smartest dog in the
world. She loved to retrieve things, including our newspaper
from the end of the driveway each morning. In some ways she
was the model child obeying virtually every command and
striving to make her parents proud.

A behavior problem emerged shortly after we moved into
our first home. Our neighbor informed us that Samantha
would jump out of our fenced-in backyard while we were at
work. Unfortunately her motive for flying the coop was to
retrieve newspapers from houses up and down our street.
Yes, our smart and previously obedient dog was now stealing
newspapers and bringing them back to our house.

As a short-term solution, we began leaving Samantha
inside the house during the day. But the problems escalated
when we came home and found one arm of our sofa nearly
chewed off. A few days later she chewed a large hole in our
living room carpet. Now we were running out of options.

After two years of nearly perfect behavior, why was our beloved family member suddenly so disobedient?

The veterinarian quickly diagnosed the problem. Separation anxiety. Samantha missed being with us and was lonely. In a dog's world, nine hours alone and isolated is an eternity. Her loneliness overflowed into bad behavior. Retrieving the neighbor's newspapers and stockpiling them in our yard was her way of winning our affection and "pleasing us" back home. When that didn't work (or was no longer an option), chewing became her addiction for overcoming the anxiety and pain. The vet gave us two options: live with it and see if it got better, or get a second dog to keep her company.

To sum up: Good motives, rooted in deep longings to be returned to her master, produced unhealthy behaviors.

Sound crazy? It's really not. It's strikingly similar to the way we behave. We are all born with a form of separation anxiety. The quiet, persistent, often unrecognized gnawing of the pain of separation from our heavenly Father produces equally unhealthy behaviors in each of us.

God's original script for mankind was a healthy, intimate, and eternal relationship with him. Man was content in his identity, his purpose, and his place. But sin tore up that script and left us bereft. Having lost our true identity, purpose, and place with the Father, we try desperately in all kinds of unhealthy ways to deal with the separation and its resulting anxiety and pain. We pursue sex, success, or significance, all in an effort to recapture what we lost.

Fortunately, even though our default script is unhealthy, God has provided a new script, starting with Jesus. Through Jesus, we are no longer separated from the Father. And through Jesus, we can live into a new script, one that God writes for us.

What distinguishes us from one another is which script we choose to live by. Will we live by a script that we try to write ourselves, trying to please ourselves and quell our own pain and anxiety? Or will we trust the script that God writes for us, and will we humbly and gratefully follow him? The wrong script motivates us to be the king of our own kingdom, using temporary and material things that we pretend will last forever (but that we know, deep down never will). In contrast, the right script motivates us to bless others with treasures that last forever.

Separation Anxiety

The Bible tells us of the condition of humans before sin was introduced to the world. Humanity is described as innocent, eternal, in direct communication and relationship with God, content and joyful in work, a caretaker or steward of God's provision, absent of negative emotions like shame and hurt, living comfortably without needs in a beautiful place, having childlike innocence (lacking God's knowledge and wisdom about good and evil), and having free-will choice to make decisions.

The Bible then tells us the consequences of sin being introduced into the world and the new script that was introduced. The bottom line? Separation. We see three key chasms or separations that result from our defiance and sin.

A LOSS OF IDENTITY AND RELATIONSHIP

Our core sense of being was altered, and our disconnection from God resulted in a fundamental shift in our understanding of identity. We were left with an identity crisis that wreaked havoc and produced unhealthy desires. Our relationship with him was severed and we became estranged. We were left confused and asking, "Who am I?"

A LOSS OF PURPOSE AND MISSION

Work became toil. The work of our hands in the garden was joyful and full of meaning and creativity. With the curse, our actions acquired a taint of frustration and futility that we hadn't known before. Instead of our activity flowing

seamlessly from our life with God, it took a different turn. We
lost the joy God intended us to experience in work. We were
left confused and asking, "What should I do?"

A LOSS OF PLACE AND ETERNAL BLISS

We lost our place in Eden and were driven out into a hostile,
uncaring world. We became captive to time and lost our
eternity of bliss with God. The joy of the perfect environment
gave way to an environment that was physically and
spiritually hostile. We were left confused, asking, "Where do
I fit?"

As a result of sin, man's contentment in and devotion
to God shifted to an elusive pursuit of accumulating,
conquering, and attaining things that will not see eternity.
We went from being God-centered to self-centered. We moved
from contentment to discontentment and from eternal life to
eternal destruction. Instead of pursuing the kingdom of God
we began to pursue the kingdom of me.

Notice how man's contentment in God's original script
gave way to an elusive pursuit of the answer to three common
questions: "Who am I created to be?" "What am I made to
do?" and "Where do I fit?"

As we will see in later chapters, the answer to these three
questions will reveal our unique personal calling—a calling
that puts the right script back into our lives with God at the
center and also equips us to help others find their way back
to God.

The Lies of Satan

In the meantime, though, Satan takes full advantage of our
separation anxiety to hold us hostage to his lies.

First, Satan twists the truth of our identity (BE) as God
intends it. He tells us that we can be the kings of our own
domains and that satisfying the desires of the moment is our
right. Like the first temptation of Jesus (making stones into

bread), Satan tries to convince us to take shortcuts to fulfill our hunger of the moment (Matthew 4:3).

Second, Satan tells us that our purpose (DO) is tied to worldly success and notoriety. The picture of Christ leaping from the temple and miraculously being unharmed would have certainly gotten some attention (Matthew 4:6). But that amazing act would have been about attention to self and not about the love and kingdom of God.

Finally, Satan tells us our best position (GO) is one of personal happiness and contentment. "You should leave your spouse for a better mate. You should leave that job for one that meets your needs more completely. Retire to an area where you can relax and enjoy yourself." These seductive lies ultimately fuel additional discontent, for we are never satisfied.

The lies of Satan always work from the outside in. He promises change through success and bread to eat and power that we can see, feel, and touch. The very longing designed as a beacon to call us to God and eternal relationship with him becomes misused as a drive and motivation for conquering and pursuing our own immortality and legacy. Some will miss the eternity they seek altogether, while others will gain life but miss the more abundant life God intends.

Satan can hijack the good that is at the core of our deep longings for eternity and immortality. Without discipline and caution, we can make the object of our desires more important than the One who is the author of our longings. While our real need is to be in relationship with the King (God) for eternity, we can spend our lives seeking to be the king here on earth. And the results of following that me-centered script will always be tragic.

The Kingdom of Me Script

For the sake of clarity, let's draw a distinction between our desires and our longings. In this book, "longings" are defined as deep-rooted emotions that shape and influence our actions but can't be satisfied on this side of eternity. Their thirst is unquenchable. Our pursuit of them is like trying to climb a nearly vertical wall of sand; we take steps but make little progress.

"Desires" are more concrete. These are things that can be pursued and conquered. Desires are tangible and you can put your hands on them. We take a step and it feels like we are making progress. But progress to what? Conquering something in this life and in our kingdom?

Make a list of everything in this life that you've won, conquered, or achieved that will have value beyond the grave. Do you see it? Most desires have a scorecard only on this side of eternity and have little value in satisfying our eternal-based longings. We must learn to shape and discipline our desires around an eternal perspective of home that transcends the temporary places we have here on earth.

Our core longings are about "being." Being in relationship with our Creator for eternity. Our desires are about defining ourselves through activity and roles. But where we get off track is when the action of our desires becomes about building our kingdoms rather than God's kingdom.

As a kid, one of my favorite games was king of the hill. It was very simple. One person, the king, was on top of a small hill seeking to maintain his or her nobility while everyone else pursued a kingship of their own by throwing the current king off the hill. The object was simple. Be the king! Why did we play? Because you wanted to be king *and* you believed you could win! This image stands as a simple yet powerful metaphor for our approach to life in our default script.

In our game of king of the hill, we desire a position of "being" the king. It's a position, place, and relationship centered on *us*. Desire provides the drive, strategy, and action to climb the hill and dethrone the current king. Desire is the "doing" that instinctively leads to the "being" in our context.

But what happens when you play a game you can never win? What happens when the fulfillment of a desire does not actually fulfill the deeper-rooted longing? What if it was impossible for you to ever be the king for more than a moment? You might play a few rounds, realize you can never win, and refocus your efforts on something more productive and satisfying.

But what if you played a few rounds and never figured out you can't win? What if you just kept trying? You might employ a new strategy, a new pursuit, a new attempt, but get the same result over and over again. Eventually you'd become increasingly frustrated, weary, and cynical. The wrong script will always produce the wrong results. Satan persistently whispers lies that keep us captive to the wrong script.

We have a deep longing. Yet we've mistakenly concluded we can work our way to kingship—to "being" who we were created to be in eternity. As a result, we've pursued the insanity of conquering but always produce the same unfulfilling results. We can become stuck in the script of seeking to become king of the hill rather than surrendering to the King of the hills.

If we are not careful and deliberate, we will believe our own insatiable longings give us a reason to pursue unhealthy earthly desires. We will pursue desires rooted in the wrong kind of *more*: doing more, accomplishing more, earning more, working more, learning more, leading more, and influencing more. Yet we will never fully satisfy these desires, and trying to do so will make us exhausted and cynical. Chasing after these desires distracts us and hijacks us from the right kind of *more*, the life of abundance that God intends for us.

The surprising key is this: we must embrace the longing we feel. Our longings can become an engine of change, shaping and defining our internal compass to constantly remind us that the home our heart longs for is deeply felt now . . . but won't be fully realized this side of eternity. This realization is a game changer.

The Kingdom of God Script

Most religions are rooted in man's desire and longing for immortality. They teach that to satisfy your deepest longing for eternity, you must work your way or prove your way into the afterlife. The forms and rules may be different, but the core approach is the same: conquer, seize, prove, sacrifice, pray, conform, and win your way to a ticket. Followers are led to believe they can eventually work their way into good graces with their creator.

It's seductive. A works-based approach to earning that eternal placement perfectly aligns with the unhealthy approach to desires discussed above. A works-based approach fuels the narcissism and me-centered approach to pursuing our desires. It's still king of the hill as we seek to claw and compete our way up to God.

We have to understand that Christianity is different and begins with God's longing for us. And even when our relationship is hindered, God is the One who works for and searches for us. We see this picture over and over in Scripture.

God calls out to Adam in the garden. He comes to Gideon in the winepress. He comes to Joseph in dreams, to Mary with an angel, and to Moses in the burning bush. He whispers Samuel's name to call the young prophet to himself. This dynamic makes Christianity unique. The first longing is God longing for us, not the other way around.

Because we are created for relationship with God, it makes sense that his longing is then imparted into our DNA. We are created in his image, and our longing has its source in his longing. It really is like a homing device or magnet with a two-way attraction.

The good news for us is that God already did the hard part. Everything needed to fulfill our longing is already accomplished. There is no quantity of work or effort we can apply on this side of eternity that will earn us time with him in the afterlife. In sending his Son, Jesus, to rescue us, he opened the way completely. Eternal life is ours for the accepting, not the creating.

What would it look like if the curse could be lifted, truly lifted? What if we could put to death the default script that we are born into in all of its futility, and instead choose the better script God has ordained for us?

What would it mean for our lives? What would it mean to be called by God without the shackles of misplaced ambitions and desires that we know so well? What would it be like to truly live in the sweet spot we were created to live in?

What would it mean for the lives of our family and friends if we could set aside our own effort and accept the amazing gift of rescue that Christ is providing for us even now? What would it mean?

We can be rescued! Not just to eternal life, but to the more abundant life here on earth that Jesus offers. But we must choose the right script! Will we live for the temporary kingdom of me—or serve willingly in the eternal kingdom of God? Jesus cries out to us, "The time has come. . . . The kingdom of heaven has come near. Repent and believe the good news!" (Mark 1:15).

Making It Personal

To embrace the truths of calling, I will abandon the earthbound kingdom of me and willingly serve in the eternal kingdom of God.

Two Kingdoms

Calling is discovered when we see our primary legacy and significance through the lens of eternity and a restored relationship with God.

Calling moves us from the captivity of the earthbound "kingship of me" to joy-filled living in the eternal kingdom of God. Taking hold of the more abundant life Jesus promises here on earth starts with choosing the right script for our motives. The amazing thing is, when we do, we find a power and a presence in our lives that can't be captured in any other way. When we lose our lives in this way, we find them in ways that touch our deepest dreams.

Calling Foundations

Clarity of calling emerges when we learn to:

1. Trust deeply the author of our story.
2. Step forward in faith, even when we cannot see clearly.
3. Abandon the earthbound kingdom of me in order to gladly serve in the eternal kingdom of God.

Visit www.personalcalling.org for supplemental resources.

CHAPTER 4

Surrendering the Leading Role

[God] has saved us and called us to a holy
life—not because of anything we have done, but
because of his own purpose and grace.

2 TIMOTHY 1:9

For several years the nighttime ritual with my youngest
son Chris was the same. It started when he was about
twelve years old and bore its fruit two years later. Growing up
in a Christian family, he had always been exposed to Jesus,
but he appropriately embraced the truth that his faith must
be his own. Chris was certain about wanting eternal life with
God but was equally certain about it being by his own faith
and decision.

During our nightly, bedtime conversations, I'd ask Chris,
"Now what must you do to be saved and spend eternity with
God and with your family?" Chris became very proficient at
answering, "Believe in Jesus, repent of my sin, confess my
desire to follow Jesus, accept Jesus as my Lord and obey
his commands, and be baptized." It wasn't a formula but
instead a sound biblical framework for weighing the costs
and a lens through which he could pursue his own faith.

Chris became keenly aware through our conversations of what each commitment meant. He could articulate in his own words what Jesus demands of us to become his followers and receive eternal life.

Dad was pleased. But something was notably missing from the list. Night after night for over a year Chris would get stuck on the phrase "accept Jesus as my Lord and obey his commands." He told me, "I'm just not sure I can do that." Chris weighed the cost just as Jesus wants his followers to do. With childlike faith and innocence, Chris resisted that commitment until he could make Jesus his personal Lord and Savior with sincerity and integrity.

Pause and think about this. The four things Chris embraced more easily—believing (in his heart), repenting (or changing his ways), confessing (proclaiming with his mouth), and being baptized—were all things that could be done without Jesus fully at the center of his life. But accepting Jesus as Lord was the game changer.

Accepting Jesus' lordship caused Jesus' disciples to stick with him when others fled. Accepting his lordship enabled his followers to refuse to renounce his name under persecution, opting instead to die in some cases tortuous deaths.

The acceptance of this lordship is a full and complete surrender to the authority, commands, and desires of another, regardless of personal impact or sacrifice. In the heavenly and spiritual realms there are only two lords: the Lord Jesus and the lord Satan; good and evil. We are told in Ephesians 6:12 that our battle is not against flesh and blood, but against the spiritual forces of evil.

This battle requires us to give up the leading role in our story, opting instead for a supporting role in the lordship of Jesus. The battle for good and evil and for our eternities is a battle of lordship. Sin is just the symptomatic outcome of our rebelliousness and failure to accept God's Son, Jesus, as our Lord and Savior.

The Cost of Lordship

Jesus warned us of the cost of making him Lord. He said, "Whoever does not carry their cross and follow me cannot be my disciple" (Luke 14:27). In Jesus' day, the cross was a symbol of pain and suffering. Following Jesus comes at a high price that requires daily surrender and sacrifice, even death in some cases. Choosing Jesus as Lord is not just a one-time decision but a lifestyle that must transform all of our behavior and actions.

We need to live new lives with new rules, new motivations, and new behaviors. But first we must weigh the cost of following Jesus. Jesus said, "Suppose one of you wants to build a tower. Won't you first sit down and estimate the cost to see if you have enough money to complete it? For if you lay the foundation and are not able to finish it, everyone who sees it will ridicule you, saying, 'This person began to build and wasn't able to finish'" (Luke 14:28–30).

Appropriately, the high cost of Jesus' lordship gave my son Chris pause. Before he surrendered to Jesus, he wrestled for over a year, weighing the costs of obedience. We too need to take Jesus' words seriously. Submitting to the lordship of Jesus is not a small commitment.

God's Calling

You might be asking yourself, what does Jesus' lordship have to do with calling?

God's work in us isn't just rescuing us from the abyss . . . it's about being called to our destiny. He calls us to himself, to rediscover who we were created to be. That redeemed core of being is the foundation for everything that follows. Everything we do and everywhere we go will be informed by the restoration of who we truly are.

Reflecting on God's call, John Ortberg writes, "A calling is very different than a quest for fulfillment. A calling, though we glamorize it, is not glamorous. It is a response to a summons. It is a kind of surrender. It is a willingness to die to the past and move to the future."[1]

God calls us personally and individually to new life. This calling is a divine invitation to be reconciled to God through Jesus Christ. Our Creator summons us to be restored to the position designed for us in eternity. In his book *The Call*, Os Guinness says, "Calling is the truth that God calls us to himself so decisively that everything we are, everything we do, and everything we have is invested with a special devotion, dynamism, and direction lived out as a response to his summons and service.... God's call has become a sure beacon ahead of me and a blazing fire within me as I have tried to figure out my way and negotiate the challenges of the extraordinary times in which we live."[2]

We are lost on our own. We need the beacon of a lighthouse to guide our steps and lead us to safe harbor. God's calling is a beacon, a voice amidst our darkness, to lead us into new life. It's the voice leading us to stop pursuing the kingship of me as a puppet under the deceptive schemes of Lord Satan, opting instead to surrender to the lordship of Jesus Christ.

Our Response

God calls us into a relationship through Jesus. Responding to God's calling is about a journey of "being" and "becoming" more like Jesus. The actions we are to take to answer his calling are rooted in a healthy relationship in submission to his lordship.

When we become convicted about surrendering to the lordship of Jesus, our natural question is "What then shall I DO?" We are naturally doers. When we were separated from God and banished to the toil of work, one of our key idols became "doing" and accomplishing. The danger in God giving us a formulaic "to do" list to be saved is that we would miss the more important point that we are entering into a new relationship, with a new Master.

In Acts 2, Peter preaches a powerful sermon on the day of Pentecost, explaining to his fellow Jews that the man they crucified, Jesus, was in truth their "Lord and Messiah" (v. 36). "When the people heard this," Luke records, "they were cut to the heart and said to Peter and the other apostles, 'Brothers, what shall we do?'" (Acts 2:37). The question, "What shall we do?" implies that they already believe. In fact, their belief prompts the question, for they sense that believing in Jesus requires more than intellectual assent.

James 2:19 says, "You believe that there is one God. Good! Even the demons believe that—and shudder." If demons believe (and clearly are not saved), then there is clearly something more than believing in Jesus that makes the difference between eternal destruction and eternal life.

Before and after the original sin that separated man from God, man believed in God. The problem causing separation was not the lack of belief, but instead the lack of lordship. It makes sense that restoring us to right relationship with God requires both belief *and* surrender to the lordship of Jesus.

This starts as a commitment to Jesus' commands, but continues as an ongoing way of life as we "continue to work out [our] salvation" (Philippians 2:12). The place of good works in the Christian life is undoubtedly controversial amongst Christians. Many argue we are saved by grace and not by works (which the Bible clearly says) and discount the role of good works in a Christian's life.

Others point to numerous verses in the Bible, including Jesus' own words, to support a place for good works. Jesus himself said, "Not everyone who says to me 'Lord, Lord,' will enter the kingdom of heaven, but only the one who does the will of my Father who is in heaven" (Matthew 7:21), and "Whoever obeys my word will never see death" (John 8:51). He also said, "Anyone who loves me will obey my teaching" and "Anyone who does not love me will not obey my teaching" (John 14:23, 24).

I personally have no problem embracing the truths that God did the hard work to make a way for us to be restored to eternal life and that through his grace he offers us salvation without our first having to complete a list of good deeds. Becoming a Christian is not like the initiation activities of a fraternity whereby we must first prove ourselves worthy of membership. That would make no sense, since the gospel is built on the understanding that we can do nothing to earn our salvation. We are completely dependent on God to make the way and extend the opportunity.

At the same time, I have no problem embracing the truth that the price of lordship and eternal life is high. It requires that we be saved from the lordship of Satan and self and delivered to the lordship of Jesus. It demands personal sacrifice and transformation. It requires faith that produces good works and deeds as an overflow of our devotion to our new Lord. Lordship must produce change and transformation in us in the form of fruit. Are we really under the lordship of Jesus if we continue to live and think as we did before coming under his authority?

Beware of a Third Script: Cultural Christianity

In western Christianity, we often devalue what it means to be a Christian. We've lowered the price of admission such that one can believe but not be transformed. We can claim to follow Jesus without obeying his commands. We can "come and see Jesus" without "coming and following him."

Cultural Christians profess belief in Jesus but show little evidence of transformed lives. Cultural Christianity removes the lordship of Jesus, often leaving a country club type of faith. In this third script, we can claim to have Jesus but still pursue the kingship of me. For a culture living at the intersection of consumerism, materialism, instant gratification, and impatience, the lure of cultural Christianity is strong.

We are losing our children because of it. They know inauthentic, tepid faith when they see it. Larry Taunton of the Fixed Point Foundation set out to find out why so many young

Christians lose their faith in college. One of the students told Taunton, "Christianity is something that if you *really* believed it, it would change your life and you would want to change [the lives] of others. I haven't seen too much of that."[3]

Choosing the Right Script

Search the Bible for yourself to discover the actions you should take to surrender to the lordship of Jesus. Look hard at your own life. Do you need to surrender to the lordship of Jesus for the first time? What are you waiting for? If you call yourself a Christian but continue to be captive to the pursuit of worldly desires prompted by the kingship of me rather than the lordship of Jesus, today can be the day to be set free!

To discover and experience God's unique personal calling and the good works he has intended for our lives, we must first accept and respond to his calling to surrender to the lordship of Jesus Christ. Only within the context of our restored relationship with God will he reveal the unique purposes and good works he has designed for our lives.

God's plan for each of us is the breaking of the me-centeredness of the curse we experienced in the garden. His call for our lives has the potential to not just give us eternal life—but to give us an earthly life of amazing abundance.

As we are restored to the identity we were created to have in Christ, we find an incredible foundation that can never be taken away. The chasms of the curse start to close, and we take our rightful place in service to a King, instead of seeking to become a king ourselves. Choosing which script to follow is our free-will choice. But only one script leads to abundant life and eternity with God.

Making It Personal

To embrace the truths of calling, I will seek daily to surrender to the lordship of Jesus.

surrendering
the Leading Role

Calling is discovered when we put the lordship of Jesus at the center of our lives.

Calling moves us from pursuing fame in our own strength to allowing the fullness of Jesus to move in us and through us to others.

Calling Foundations

Clarity of calling emerges when we learn to:

1. Trust deeply the author of our story.
2. Step forward in faith, even when we cannot see clearly.
3. Abandon the earthbound kingdom of me in order to gladly serve in the eternal kingdom of God.
4. Submit to the lordship of Jesus.

Visit www.personalcalling.org for supplemental resources.

CHAPTER 5

Redefining Success

And God placed all things under [Jesus']
feet and appointed him to be head over everything
for the church, which is his body, the fullness of
him who fills everything in every way.

EPHESIANS 1:22–23

I spent fifteen years working as an engineer at the Division of Naval Reactors, one of the greatest engineering organizations in the world. Naval Reactors was responsible for every aspect of naval nuclear propulsion, including design, operations, maintenance, repair, and decommissioning of nuclear ships.

When Naval Reactors celebrated its fiftieth year of operation, it had clocked over 100,000,000 miles of safe nuclear ship operation via hundreds of nuclear submarines and aircraft carriers. These ships sailed the world over in peacetime and wartime, carrying operating nuclear plants in and near population centers.

Imagine the consequences of just one nuclear accident aboard a ship. Not only would it immediately impact the people involved, but it would have ripple effects ranging from the environmental impact to our national security, as other ships might be recalled and unable to fulfill their mission.

Hired as a young, energetic college graduate, at first I did not fully comprehend that our driving mission was safety. Thankfully, a seasoned veteran of the organization brought the concept home to me in a simple way. He suggested that I visit a nuclear ship prior to departure and spend several hours observing sailors with their families as they hugged and kissed their children goodbye, possibly never to return. My mentor asked me to look into the tear-streaked faces of those spouses and children and weigh the magnitude of our responsibility in bringing those sailors home safely. While war might not occur during their time away, the nuclear reactor propelling their ship could wreak terrible devastation. Our mission was to bring those sailors home safely to their waiting family members. When I embraced the truth that my work and my responsibilities could make the difference between celebration or heartbreak for countless families, my viewpoint of my mission changed radically, and I began to own the seriousness of it.

We need to be reminded from time to time of why we do what we do and how we will measure success in the scorecard of eternity. The right view of success and mission is vital in shaping a healthy journey toward our personal calling.

Changing Our Thinking

In his letter to the Ephesians, Paul says that the church is to be the fullness of Jesus who fills everything in every way (1:23). Create a mental image of what it looks like for one thing to completely fill and engulf another thing, leaving no crack or crevice untouched. Think of water filling an aquarium, completely surrounding and engulfing every object within the tank, including the rocks, the coral, and the artificial castle; 100 percent of the available surface area contacts the water. In a similar way, Paul says that the church is like water, permeating every crack and crevice of society, leaving nothing untouched by the fullness of Jesus.

Hear that again. We are to be like the water, leaving nothing untouched by the love of God.

Sound impossible? That's because of our experience and trust in the ways of the physical world. Think of the most impactful organizations in recent history. You might consider corporations like Apple, Google, Amazon, eBay, Microsoft, and Ford Motor Company. Combine their collective skills, capacities, and abilities. Add in the rest of the businesses in America. Multiply that by 1,000,000. Could the resultant entity "fill everything in every way?" Not a chance.

Yet we are promised that the church, in all its shortcomings, has that capacity. God gave it a sacred design with a sacred plan. The church is the most powerful movement in the history of the world with the capacity to fill everything in every way with the fullness of Christ!

That is a game changer, but here is the challenging part. Do you believe that the potential of your personal calling is connected to the fullness of Jesus in your community? That God's perfect plan for your life in this generation is about the fullness of Christ touching you and the people around you deeply?

If so, then you need to be a vibrant part of the church. Forget preconceived notions for a moment; set aside your vision of "church" with any negative association. Just take God at his word—the church is the instrument of the fullness of Jesus intersecting with us.

When seen in that light, calling and church are inseparable.

The church's potential, as Jesus intended it, is not bound by our personal, negative experiences or history with the local church. Our skepticism comes from not really believing the church can do and accomplish what the Bible says it can. That somehow the church doesn't matter or is outdated. That the power and work of the Holy Spirit, so evident in the early church, is somehow no longer alive in and through us. Down deep many of us have become convinced we are part of a losing team. This results in our giving less than our full devotion to our local faith community.

Our skepticism also comes from seeing individual and parachurch organizations that seem to be more effective in mission than the more traditional "church" in their community. Here we need to break down barriers and rethink what church really is. It's not just the individual organization . . . it is the people God has called to himself, which even at the local level may be a lot of different organizations.

Most of us want to be part of something bigger than ourselves, a compelling vision and work of God. We must embrace the truth of what the church can and should be. When we do, the fullness of Christ flowing into every crack and cranny of society will happen faster and more comprehensively than we ever could have imagined.

Living in Common as God's Family

Jesus' design for the church is that we live in common, taking care of one another's needs, functioning as a family. Regardless of our position and gifting, we are to do whatever it takes to support the whole and one another. From holding babies to doing life together, from greeting newcomers to financially supporting the unemployed among us, we are all connected as the body of Christ, the church. We do whatever it takes to support one another.

Living in common as a family, sharing and caring for one another, is intended to be a 24/7 lifestyle. Jesus calls for our first fruits—the best of our time, talent, and treasure—to be invested in one another.

Read Acts 2:42–47 and look specifically at what the early church family did and what the results were. They devoted themselves to learning, fellowship (including eating together), prayer, sharing, and taking care of one another; in other words, they committed to regular, ongoing life-on-life. A simple picture of biblical community, the body of Christ being

54

the church, investing their first fruits in living in common. The results? God added to their numbers daily. This was not a one-time fluke, but rather a pattern we see throughout the early church and a picture of what a community of faith is meant to be.

Survey the Bible looking specifically at strategies for outreach and evangelism. You will find that the single most prominent pattern for growth is the fellowship of Christians described in Acts 2. This is a paradox. By taking care of one another and modeling healthy family inside the movement, outsiders want to become insiders. Those far from God instinctively want what those close to God actively experience. A movement emerges, fueling itself with biblical community, wrapped around the good news of Jesus as the secret formula for the expanding impact.

Read Acts 2 again. This time focus on what you don't read. Nothing about profound strategies of organizational alignment, clarity of vision, great preaching, outreach, marketing, strategic planning, or hiring of gifted staff. I confess my personal testimony of Acts 2 is all too often: "They devoted themselves to vision clarity, organizational alignment, healthy teams, geographically based small groups, great preaching, monster outreach events, massive marketing campaigns, world class children's ministry, the best music in town, leadership development, new sites, and the latest growth strategy to break the next barrier. Some of the believers came together weekly for an excellent Sunday morning show; others opted for overbooked schedules of travel sports and long work hours to pay increasing debt, leaving no margin for living in common. With divorce, addiction, and crime rates similar to society at large, outsiders mocked the church, wondering why they should be part of something so judgmental, hypocritical, and irrelevant. Rather than praising God for the abundance of blessing and being the fullness of Christ in everything and in every way, church members spent their time praying for deliverance from the same crazy, empty lives as their outsider friends. When numbers were not added daily, they looked for the next silver bullet to catalyze growth and make the church more relevant. They desperately sought to *do* church without *being* the church."

In God's wisdom the church is perfectly designed to allow believers living in common to become the fullness of Christ to the world in everything and in every way. Yes, preaching and teaching are important and personal witnessing is important, but it's the substance of what happens in our community— the gospel in radical practice within the church day to day—that profoundly attracts those far from God.

Do we fall short in being all that Jesus intends? Yes. But that doesn't change the truth that the local church is his chosen strategy for deploying his followers to carry the fullness of himself into every corner of society. We can dislike our shortcomings in doing church, but we can't disown it without being in rebellion against its Founder.

Embracing the Blemishes and the Beauty

The church becomes more beautiful and more complete as more and more people engage and pursue the fullness of Christ through the use of their unique gifts and service. Our gifts are not our own. They are truly on loan for the benefit of the whole family of God and our community at large.

This isn't about strengthening a local organization, though that may happen. This is about spreading the fullness of Jesus in our generation.

In the scorecard of eternity, our personal calling will always be incomplete outside the context of being an active family member in the local church. If we are not disciplined in our daily, personal practices as demonstrated in the Acts 2 church, why would we expect to live abundantly in the sweet spot of calling God designed for us?

Could you pursue a personal calling while ignoring the church? Yes. We can choose to be planes without airports, but our effectiveness will be limited. More importantly, that path represents a misunderstanding about why God gave us a unique set of gifts and calling in the first place, and ultimately it keeps the church from being all that he intends. We will never fully experience what God has planned if we choose the Lone Ranger path.

Let me encourage you to recommit yourself to being fully devoted to a community of Christ followers, regardless of what form it takes (i.e., small group, missional community, traditional church, megachurch, etc.). Not as a martyr but as one who chooses to live the Christian life in common with others. Be one who chooses daily to bless others in small things. One who can model a life of sharing regardless of the shortcomings of a local expression of church. One who can model and become a spark for others to be devoted to one another.

Roll up your sleeves and embrace your local church or diligently pursue finding one where you and your family can be fully devoted to living in common as the body of Christ. Don't be lukewarm. Devote yourself to being all-in regardless of the church's quirks and blemishes. Make a difference daily where you are. The good works God has called you to do will be multiplied and made more effective if you are surrounded by a community of faith.

Let the devotion and community of the local church release the true potential of your individual calling.

The Need for Refreshing

That being said, don't settle. God periodically brings amazing change to his church for the sake of it being the fullness of his love to the current generation. We must break out of our limited and incomplete thinking of the church as just a building or institution. Peter Drucker, the father of modern management, said: "The number of years has been shrinking during which an employing institution can expect to stay successful. This period was never very long. Historically, very few businesses were successful for as long as thirty years in a row. To be sure, not all businesses ceased to exist when they ceased to do well. But the ones that survived beyond thirty years usually entered into a long period of stagnation—and only rarely did they turn around again and once more become successful growth businesses."[1]

The church is not immune from the organizational life cycle that Drucker describes. For over 2000 years, local churches have perpetuated the movement of Christianity in thirty-year cycles. Consider the fact that not a single first-century church is still in existence, and yet every church today can trace its roots to a first-century church. This isn't a bad thing! Each generation of believers works with God uniquely to fulfill God's purpose in their time and place. We need to be open and flexible to where God is calling us next.

If we, as individual disciples, are grounded in the foundation of being who we are in Christ, we'll dynamically influence the organizations and processes to which we are devoted in healthy ways. By being engaged in the church and pursuing our journey of calling, we'll naturally bring change to our local church—just by being who we are.

It is not the brick and mortar of our buildings that has propelled the movement of Christianity for centuries. It is the simplicity of individuals being disciples of Jesus, in all his fullness, wherever we are and wherever we go, making new disciples along the way.

Living Water

During trips to Israel, I'm always fascinated by the ongoing archeological work and amazed at how little of it has actually been completed. Although ancient buildings typically lie in ruins, their remnants give clues into life and priorities in the past.

On a recent trip we stumbled upon an active archeological site along the Sea of Galilee. This site is of particular interest in learning about life in Jesus' day as he would have visited it and its synagogue many times. So you can imagine our excitement at stumbling onto this active "crime scene."

At the heart of each Jewish community were a synagogue and mikvah baths for ritual and physical purification. There are two kinds of mikvah baths: those filled by workers using water collected from rain; and those dynamically filled from active, running, fresh springs. Those from fresh springs were of utmost importance, and that kind of water was referred to as "living water."

In John 4:14, Jesus told the woman at the well, "Whoever drinks the water I give them will never thirst. Indeed, the water I give them will become in them a spring of water welling up to eternal life." Jesus' message, his life, his death, and his resurrection are the source from which eternal life springs. We are called to take this living water into our communities, pouring it out and letting it permeate into every crack and crevice of society.

As we approached the newly uncovered baths, we could literally hear fresh, spring water flowing through stone channels built two thousand years ago. With excitement, our young archeologist guide explained how she had cleared mud and debris from the channel to restart its flow of water for the first time in nearly two thousand years. What was stagnant and dead was now alive and flowing again.

This is a picture of what God wants to do in us. The big idea of calling (and of the church) is the fullness of Jesus in us, through us, and to others.

Metaphorically, we have a choice to make. Will we be "rivers of living water" (John 7:38) to flow through and fill every corner of society? Or will we be like that dirt and debris that keeps the living water from reaching others we are called to reach? Or even worse, will we be a bit of water separated from the channel—never making much of a difference at all?

When a group of people desperately pursuing God and his calling come together, they turn their individual contributions of living water into a powerful flowing river. This is what God wants the church to be: the fullness of Jesus in us, flowing through us, to this generation.

It's you and I fully devoted to calling, experiencing the love of God deeply in our lives and in the lives of our families. It's you and I fully devoted to each other, living in common, pursuing God and calling together in an amazing network of extended family. It's you and I fully devoted to others, being the fullness of Jesus, letting that living water flow through us to feed the baths of our community.

God's call is all about bringing life to us and through us. When we see carrying the fullness of Jesus as our mission, we stop focusing on our individual achievements and worldly success. Instead, we define success in terms of eternity, and in the context of a faith community, we serve as a channel for carrying God's abundance and fullness to an incredibly dry and dusty world!

Making It Personal

To embrace the truths of calling, I will embrace God's primary mission for me to carry the fullness of Jesus to every corner of society. I will also devote myself to living in common as a family member in a healthy, local community of faith.

redefining
Success

Calling is discovered and finds its context within the church's mission: to carry the fullness of Jesus into every corner of society.

Calling helps us to redefine success. Instead of striving for individual success and worldly gain, we find our success and purpose in carrying the fullness of Jesus to the world. Our unique gifting and good works become God's way of accomplishing his mission. Calling isn't about ego. It's about giving ourselves away. A healthy church gives us an amazing network to do just that.

Calling is discovered through living in common with a local community of faith.

Calling moves us from isolation to being part of a vibrant and unending family. We weren't meant to walk this journey alone. Friendship and the support of community are a necessary part of calling, both for our encouragement and our ability to encourage and support others.

Calling Foundations

Clarity of calling emerges when we learn to:

1. Trust deeply the author of our story.
2. Step forward in faith, even when we cannot see clearly.
3. Abandon the earthbound kingdom of me in order to gladly serve in the eternal kingdom of God.
4. Submit to the lordship of Jesus.
5. Embrace our mission to carry the fullness of Jesus to every corner of society.
6. Live in common with a healthy, local community of faith.

Visit www.personalcalling.org for supplemental resources.

CHAPTER 6

Owning My Part

> Then Jesus came to them and said, "All
> authority in heaven and on earth has been given to
> me. Therefore go and make disciples of all nations,
> baptizing them in the name of the Father and of the
> Son and of the Holy Spirit, and teaching them to
> obey everything I have commanded you. And surely
> I am with you always, to the very end of the age."
>
> MATTHEW 28:18-20

More than two hundred years ago, George Washington led a tattered colonial army through a series of devastating losses, a brutal winter, and extreme discouragement to victory against the greatest military force in the world. How did he do it? How in the world did the Revolutionary War result in a win for anyone but Britain?

Washington's brilliant strategy and leadership were crucial. His knowledge of the terrain that he acquired in the role of surveyor as a young man played a part. Scholars could point to many other factors that influenced the eventual outcome. But a key ingredient to American military success was a simple and visceral element. It was proxy.

Proxy is defined as "the power of a person authorized to act as the substitute for another." In terms of power, focus, and personal responsibility, proxy seems like an effective transfer of power, but played out in the real world, it can often result in potentially harmful loss.

The British soldiers were there as a proxy of the British Empire. Thousands of miles from home, they traveled across an ocean, were deployed, and fought battles representing the power and interest of England. They were professionals. They were well trained and supplied. They were the sword of Britain at the height of the British Empire's military power. Yet they lacked an ingredient that ragtag colonial soldiers possessed. They were there with an institutional proxy, not a personal proxy.

For the rebels, this wasn't just a military exercise. There was no institutional proxy; they were fighting for a compelling personal cause. They "owned" the risk and reward of the Revolution in a way that simply wasn't possible for the British troops. They took up arms against an overwhelming foe to protect their farms and families. They fought battles from behind trees on their personal property and in the cities they called home. Their mission was compelling; it was their heartbeat and focus.

Put yourself in their shoes for a moment. Does it change your perspective of an exhausting forced march when you are marching to save your home? Does your heart in that situation give you strength for one more step before you collapse? Do you load your gun a little bit faster when you face the desperation of insuring your family's safety? Do you fire with more focus when your own home and children are in the balance?

The proxy of the British soldiers was nothing to sneer at; they were a daunting military force. But the Revolutionary soldiers had an urgency of spirit that was unmatchable. This difference in institutional versus personal proxy is at the core of why underdogs with a cause have defeated mighty foes again and again throughout history.

Democratic Republics

With the colonial victory came the founding of the government of the United States of America. We are a democratic republic, which means we assign our proxy to elected officials to do the work of governing. We are represented by the president, congress, justices, governors, and a host of officials. We give them our proxy to handle a variety of functions. Part of this is necessary for practical reasons, but we also shouldn't be surprised that politicians holding proxy for our families aren't as passionate about our individual needs as we are.

Anytime we give up personal proxy to institutional proxy, we incrementally dilute the passion and impulse that propels the larger movement. This is the natural lifecycle of many organizations. How do giants become giants? And how do giants fall? They start out messy and ragtag. They are built on zealous radicals sold out to a cause and taking ownership via their own proxy. Not surprisingly, they often experience explosive growth and success.

As the movement or organization matures, personal proxy slowly gives way to organizational proxy. The organization must figure out how to reestablish the original, organic impulse that gave the movement life, or it will face eventual death. The less active we are as thoughtful citizens, the bigger our national problems become. You could make the case that as a nation, we've given too much of our proxy away.

In this sense, it could be said, "So goes the republic, so goes the church." We've bought into the republic form of church. We show up and give our financial support and proxy to paid full-time professionals to represent us as God's voice in the world.

This is a mistake. God never intended the institution to replace the power and intimacy of individual proxy. Our Ephesians 2:10 unique calling is an intimate and personal proxy never meant to be given away or delegated to someone else. The delegation stopped with Jesus.

The power and brilliance of God's design for the church is a relational community, focused on mission and functioning like a family, with every member owning and living out their personal proxy. The support of the family comes not through delegating or giving up one's personal proxy to an institutional proxy, but rather by every member discovering and engaging and living out their personal proxy. Every member both living in common and living deployed.

God seeks to make it personal with each of us by giving us a unique sweet spot and purpose that is the handiwork of his creativity. This calling works hand in hand with the urgency we feel for the people we know by name. The church is part of the plan, but no institution or nonprofit will substitute for our day-to-day passion and personal proxy.

Proxy and the Church

Ephesians 4:11–13 says, "Christ himself gave the apostles, the prophets, the evangelists, the pastors and teachers, to equip his people for works of service, so that the body of Christ may be built up until we all reach unity in the faith and in the knowledge of the Son of God and become mature, attaining to the whole measure of the fullness of Christ." We are each uniquely gifted by Jesus for the benefit of the church in completing his mission here on earth. This isn't an institutional proxy; we have a personal proxy from the CEO of the church.

What will we do with it?

In John 20:21, Jesus says, "Peace be with you! As the Father has sent me, I am sending you." He did not say, "I'm sending the ones you delegate your proxy to." He said, "I'm sending *you!*" In the context of living in common and supporting one another, we all have missions to accomplish.

In terms of life mission and God's purposes, we must become the colonial soldier who is fighting with passion for our home and family and neighbors and city. For no one will see our context with the perspective that we do. No one else will have the opportunities to move and speak in our story like we will. No one will have the passion we do to get the job done. No other approach could carry the fullness of Christ in everything and in every way into every nook and cranny of society.

What would happen if we all, in our contexts, brought the heart of church with us into the various corners of life? What if we all assumed the role of missionary, deployed by our local church to be the fullness of Christ in everything and in every way, as we touch the lives of people around us? What if we assumed the role of a pastor in our unique context? What if in our living in common, as a family of believers, we went out on daily missions to the world? What would prevent us from keeping our proxy close, held as a sacred calling of influence? What if we took this struggle personally and decided to fight for our own home turf?

That idea is inspiring, and it should be. But there is danger here as well. Imagine what would happen if every single Revolutionary soldier decided to go his own way. Instead of reporting back to their unit, they kept going on their own. No army, no militia, no coordinating with General Washington . . . just an enormous number of individuals fighting the British army as they thought best. Would America have won the war? Even the passion and energy of personal proxy would not have sufficed. Instead, the community and organization of the Revolutionary Army was necessary to multiply their effectiveness as individual soldiers.

This is one reason we need to function as a healthy family, united and connected via the church. Don't give up your proxy. But know that the community of faith can strengthen you, encourage you, and help you stay on mission.

Unintended Consequences of Giving Our Proxy Away

If Christianity is the greatest movement in the history of the world (a fact which few people would argue against), then why does this movement seem hindered in the US? I believe it's a direct consequence of two mistakes. One, we withhold the power and full influence of our calling and proxy by not being part of the church. Two, we misunderstand how church ought to function. We too often give away our personal proxies to the institutional element of churches and nonprofits.

Let me explain this dynamic by exploring the elements of movements. If you study the core elements of any kind of movement—from the church to the growth of terror cells—you will see at least four distinct elements as shown below. These elements work in harmony like a flywheel. As the core message is delivered via people and amplified and further expanded through a community or tribe, the resulting impact serves to further propel the message.

The elements are: a core message, a tribe, a delivery channel, and an impact. As the cycle repeats, it picks up steam and a movement emerges.

FLYWHEEL OF MOVEMENT

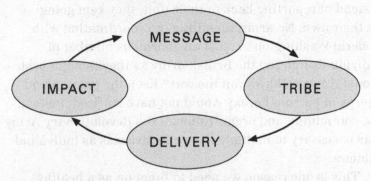

As an example, let's look at terrorist cells.

The Message/Cause: The message is, "Kill the infidels!" It's so simple that even those who are not part of the movement know the message.

The Tribe: The organizational structure of this community is known as decentralized cells—a "starfish" organization (i.e., you can cut off an arm and it grows it back) that can covertly go under cover and exist virtually anywhere at any time. You will not find a corporate headquarters on the top floor of a skyscraper. However, if you could visit these decentralized cells anywhere in the world, you'd find an incredibly strong alignment and devotion to the core message and cause.

The Delivery Channel: The message is delivered by its followers, who are connected to the community via decentralized cells and who are sold out to its message and cause.

The Impact: Fear, death, and destruction.

Notice the flywheel. As the impact of fear and executions expand, additional extremists are drawn to the cause, further fueling the growth and expansion of new cells and increased fear and destruction. The cycle feeds on itself. That's what happens in movements.

Using this model, let's look at how Jesus intended the church to function.

The Message/Cause: The message is divine love expressed in Jesus. He died that we might have life and be reconciled to God, both here and eternally in heaven.

The Tribe: The tribe is a local community of faith, the church. The genius of God's design is that the power of biblical community—with disciples living in common—is evangelistic in and of itself.

The Delivery Channel: The delivery is made by disciples whose lives have been transformed and changed. We experience "living water" and can't help sharing it with others in word and deed. We are given a unique, sacred proxy in the form of a personal calling to help equip us to live deployed into every crack and cranny of society, to be living examples of and witnesses to the message by which we've been personally transformed, a message that we are compelled to share. We deploy where the institution can't go itself.

The Impact: The impact is the transformation of hearts and lives. We experience redemption, salvation, and eternal life. Our lives become abundant.

The transformation in our own hearts and lives becomes the fuel and motivation for sharing with others. The passion of our personal proxy leads us to carry the love and fullness of Jesus into everything in every way. As we live deployed, we carry the message in a real and relevant way to the world around us. If we don't do that, effectively giving that proxy away, the focus becomes simply the church and the steeple and all its people who gather for an hour a week.

If we mishandle our proxy, we will stunt the movement dynamics of Christianity. In functioning like a republic and giving away our individual proxies, we've functionally and unintentionally combined the delivery channel and the tribe. Instead of the individual disciple being the primary channel for communicating the message, we've allowed the organization of church to take on that role. This results in Sunday morning services becoming the primary distribution channel. That would be like Starbucks only serving coffee at their corporate headquarters, one day a week.

In combining the primary delivery channel and the tribe, we become less effective at both living in common *and* at living deployed. We dilute what is intended. The disciple as the primary delivery mechanism is accomplished by living deployed. If you give that proxy away, it becomes less intimate, less personal, and less powerful.

You might be the world's greatest servant to others, but you will lose your joy if you are not also doing what you were made to do. That's what happens to us when we give our proxy away and confuse the roles of the delivery channel (a disciple living deployed) and the tribe (the church providing an environment for living in common).

The Need to Align Church, Calling, and Support

Let our devotion be like the devotion of the early church. "They devoted themselves to the apostles' teaching and to fellowship, to the breaking of bread and to prayer. . . . and the Lord added to their number daily those who were being saved" (Acts 2:42, 47b). Devotion is always *to* something. In devoting themselves to *doing* the right things in biblical community, they were *being* the church in its intended design. The discipline of doing right things produces the fruit of being the church Jesus intended.

Instead of focusing on an hour a week as an isolated activity, churches must become incubators of calling. They must create environments where discipleship happens organically. The processes of the institution should work to empower personal proxy. We should be seeking to work with God collectively to train, equip, release, and amplify our individual contributions to mission.

It should also be an opportunity for us to support each other in vibrant and practical ways.

The local church, regardless of its form (from house church to mega-church to missional faith community), requires laborers willing to do whatever it takes to live in full devotion to each other. We are to serve one another as a family, meeting internal needs, and we are to engage in unique good works prepared beforehand by God in order to live missionally and serve the world.

Do you see it? Our proxy calls us to serve in two roles simultaneously.

First, we support one another, doing whatever is needed to be a healthy family, helping our brothers and sisters in Christ be the very best they can be.

Second, we pursue God's unique personal calling for us with all of our hearts.

This is success: leveraging the synergy of calling within a community of like-minded believers, our local church. Only in connection to the church can we take the fullness of Jesus to all corners of society. Only within it can we truly experience the fullness of Jesus in us, through us, and to this generation!

The Questions of Calling

If you characterized the heart of the great leaders of the faith, the Hebrews 11 list for example, what do they have in common? Perhaps you could reframe this question personally: "Will I go wherever, to work with whomever, whenever, doing whatever God asks, regardless of the consequences?"

Abraham could answer "Yes" to that question. So could Joseph and Ruth and Elijah and many others. What about us? Take a moment and answer these questions as honestly as possible.

Am I willing to move and go wherever God wants me to go?

Think about that. Are we willing to quit the current job? Sell the house? Move the family? What if it were a situation like Abram's and we're not sure what the destination is yet? Could we give notice and prepare to leave in the way that he did?

Am I willing to work with whomever God wants me to work?

It might not involve speaking at a conference with lights and an enthusiastic crowd with our name on the screen. It might involve loving people we don't like, that we might have some issues with, who come at life in a way that makes no sense to us and who are hard to empathize with. What if our situation is like Jeremiah's and our entire ministry is standing in the rubble, preaching to a generation who simply will not respond?

Am I willing to go whenever God asks me to go?

God's timing is his own. Are we willing to go now? The possible objections are all but infinite. We don't have our degree yet! Or do we feel like we need the children to get off to college first? What if he calls and we're just not ready? Are we in a place where we could say "yes" in an extravagant way immediately? On the other side of the "whenever" is this: are we willing to wait? Like Joshua, are we willing to show patience for an entire generation and not step into full leadership until we are old?

Am I willing to do whatever God asks me to do, regardless of consequences?

Calling doesn't always make sense at first. It doesn't always make sense in the middle, and it can be frustrating and seem like too much to bear at the end. What if our crowning moment of calling was similar to Jesus' ministry on earth? Instead of riding off into the sunset with good things in tow, what if we find ourselves in Gethsemane, facing a price that is just too high to pay? Even if everything in you is screaming, "find another way!" are you willing to lay down your life if God desires it? Are you willing to let Judas kiss you on the cheek? Are you willing to pay the ultimate price for his plan?

Those are hard questions. They are. Even the most committed of us will hesitate on one or all of them if we're honest. Our tendency is to start asking questions of our own. Could we wait a year to get ready? Are there vacation days? Is there good housing there? How are the schools for our children? Is there a retirement plan? We'll have friends, won't we? If I pay this price, I'll see amazing things happening immediately, right?

The even harder question is this:

How can I expect God to send me and use me if I'm not really willing to go?

Do we really believe he can take care of us? Do we really believe if we sacrifice things for him it will be worth it? Do we trust that God knows what he is doing? Are we willing to surrender control when it comes to the path of our lives?

If we can't say yes in these ways, how can we expect our story to be anything but a story that never really gets told? How can God use us if we lift our comfort above his purpose? Is there a connection between the 99.9 percent of us that never fully and completely engage and our ability to really say yes?

It is human nature to worry or to conjure up the worst-case scenario as we consider relinquishing control of the path of our lives. The paradox and irony of calling are that when we pour out our hearts completely, we find ourselves full and our needs met.

It is fair to say that provision will probably not come in the way we expected. But at the end of the day, it will be so much better than pursuing our dreams of security and safe passage. Following the "yes" into God's calling will not be an easy path. It will not be a comfortable path, but it will be a path filled with joy that you will never regret when your story is told in full.

Making It Personal

To embrace the truths of calling, I will take responsibility for the unique personal calling and role God has given me within my family of faith.

owning
My Part

Calling is discovered when we take personal responsibility for the unique role Jesus gives us.

Calling leads us to discover and engage our unique gifting in good works, never delegating our proxy to a church or institution. That requires courage and a real moment of decision when we see it and decide not to hide anymore.

Calling Foundations

Clarity of calling emerges when we learn to:

1. Trust deeply the author of our story.
2. Step forward in faith, even when we cannot see clearly.
3. Abandon the earthbound kingdom of me in order to gladly serve in the eternal kingdom of God.
4. Submit to the lordship of Jesus.

5. Embrace our mission to carry the fullness of Jesus to every corner of society.

6. Live in common with a healthy, local community of faith.

7. Take personal responsibility of the unique role Jesus gives us.

Visit www.personalcalling.org for supplemental resources.

CHAPTER 7

Trusting the Guide

I will ask the Father, and he will give you another advocate to help you and be with you forever.

JOHN 14:16

Wait.
Patiently.

That probably wasn't what they expected.

Jesus appeared to his friends after conquering death and rising from the grave. He returns to activate his church and give his followers their marching orders. He gives them a mission to go into the world, making disciples to the ends of the earth. His plan is in place and ready to break forth, bearing fruit and multiplying.

His next play? "Wait." He tasks them with staying in Jerusalem. Wait? Why? Waiting seems to contradict Jesus' orders to "go." How could waiting be vitally important to the mission?

They are told to wait and receive the secret weapon that will make this new movement unstoppable and set this small group of Christ followers apart from those who are far from God. They are promised a special power from the Holy Spirit. A supernatural power that has parted seas, allowed underdogs to conquer powerful enemies, multiplied a few fish to feed five thousand men, and empowered faithful leaders of humble beginnings to step out and do the remarkable.

It is the same power that raised Jesus from the dead. It is the same power that eventually propelled the gospel message far beyond Jerusalem. And it is the same power that will help us navigate the fog in our lives, embrace our unique role in the church, and live deployed, engaging our unique good works and pursuing holiness in becoming more like Jesus.

What are the implications of this initial call for the disciples to wait? To be blunt, it means this: We will fail in our journey of calling without the indwelling of the Holy Spirit. We simply can't do it alone. We need help. We need this power. We need the Holy Spirit.

Many principles in this book will work for unbelievers. Self-discovery and assessment are valuable aids for success in career and relationships. The truths that we are unique and that life can be filled with purpose can be embraced by unbelievers. But if we stop there, we face a real danger.

If the highest purpose of personal calling becomes self-improvement and a vehicle for success, we can become focused on self in unhealthy ways. We can become our own idols and eventually our own worst enemy. Consider people like Michael Jackson, Steve Jobs, and Vince Lombardi, brilliantly achieving success after success, yet leaving behind a swath of tragic personal destruction in their wake.

Now imagine each of those people centered in the power and leading of the Holy Spirit. Greatness can still be present, but with a loving and God-centered life, how much more impact could these individuals have had, especially in their relationships with those closest to them?

Without submitting to the lordship of Christ, without the personal guiding of the Holy Spirit, there is something missing even in the sharpest personal focus or the most resounding professional success.

This chapter takes a fresh look at the vital role the Holy Spirit plays in our pursuit of personal calling.

Empowered Ambassadors

An ambassador is an authorized representative and messenger to a people group with a special purpose. The apostle Paul says, "We are therefore Christ's ambassadors, as though God were making his appeal through us" (2 Corinthians 5:20). We are instruments through which the gospel message is shared with the world.

Earlier, we discussed the purpose of the church: to be the fullness of Christ in everything and in every way in our communities. The idea is completeness, like water filling a container to overflowing.

Now consider the Holy Spirit, dwelling in us, as the answer to that challenge related to calling. The Holy Spirit can fill everything in every way. In his mysteriously complex yet simple plan, God makes us his ambassadors. He gives us his indwelling Holy Spirit who can fill everything in every way.

He seeks first to do a transforming and sanctifying work in us so that he can more powerfully work through us. Even as we are an active work in progress, we become his ambassadors to others.

You see, there is just no way we can do it on our own in our own strength and power. It's impossible. Yet that's the approach we try over and over again while the Holy Spirit waits patiently for our feeble hands to surrender control.

Personal Advocate

The Bible calls the Holy Spirit our Advocate and Counselor. Jesus said, "I will ask the Father, and he will give you another advocate to help you and be with you forever—the Spirit of Truth. The world cannot accept him, because it neither sees him nor knows him. But you know him, for he lives with you and will be in you" (John 14:16–17).

Pause for a moment and think about the advocates you've had in your life. These may be parents, friends, teachers, or possibly a boss, an attorney, or a coach. Consider what they did for you and how they did it.

At the age of thirty, I found myself with way more responsibility than a person that age would normally have. In providing oversight of an industrial complex with thousands of employees, I was asked regularly, "How did you get to that position at such a young age?" When I looked beyond my unique gifts and drive, the answer was simple: I had the raw abilities and talents needed, but far more important were the strong advocates cheering and helping me along the way.

Bill Shirley and Souren Hanessian were senior leaders in our organization, years ahead of me in experience. They had successfully walked the path I wanted to travel. They believed in me and became strong advocates and proponents of me and my future. Their words of endorsement to other key leaders were vital in my journey toward the promotions I received. At the same time, they had earned my trust and could continually speak into my life, highlighting strengths and weaknesses in a way others could not.

Our earthly advocates are blessings, but even at their very best they have limitations. They are not available 24/7; they have their own lives and aspirations and problems to tend to. We get a small fraction of their actual time and energy. While their best intentions are to help us, their counsel is fallible and may or may not be the best advice for us.

Now consider the qualifications of the Holy Spirit:

- Working 24/7 with on-demand access
- Constantly looking out for God's best interests for us, and whispering in our ears
- Encouraging when comfort is needed
- Convicting when accountability is needed
- Guiding when direction is needed
- Interceding when we simply have no words to maneuver the chaos
- Exhibiting all the characteristics of the best, truest friend
- Just waiting for us to give over control

The leaders of the early church were utterly reliant on the indwelling power of the Holy Spirit. Peter, Paul, and the other apostles could not have comprehended their calling in the absence of their Advocate. It would be like imagining marriage without a spouse.

It's time to become equipped and empowered in the way Jesus designed for us. It's time to truly embrace the same Advocate who has been active and alive since the beginning of the church and is still with us today, ready to captain our ship.

Unique Gifts and Calling

So how does the role and presence of the Holy Spirit relate to personal calling?

We receive clarity on our unique calling through the guidance of the Holy Spirit. Assessment tools, interviews, and experiential learning exercises are all helpful, but the role of the Holy Spirit trumps everything else.

Our personal calling is a sacred gift from God, not earned by anything we've done but created freely by the hand of God. First Corinthians 12:1, 4–11 says the Holy Spirit is the one who distributes our individual gifts for the benefit of the common good of the church. He distributes them as he determines according to the will of God.

If you could pick just one action to discover your personal calling, choose this: listen to and learn from the Holy Spirit.

The World's Greatest Tour Guide

As we seek to listen for the clues our divine story reveals about who we are, remember that our tour guide for the journey is the one who made us. He is the one who calls us to himself and to a life of good works. He is the one who fearfully and wondrously knit us together in our mother's womb.

God already sees the complete story of our lives with perfect clarity. He is the one who leaves a string of clues for us to discover, and he whispers into our ear the divine mysteries of who we uniquely are through the people who intersect our story every day. Call on him to be the guide for your journey. Invite him daily to show you the clues.

I'm reminded of the National Museum of the Marine Corps, run mostly by volunteer war veterans. My favorite part of the museum is the Iwo Jima exhibit, and I can still hear the voice of our guide during my last visit. He was a World War II vet whose company stormed the shores of Iwo Jima. He was passionate. His story was compelling. I learned and retained more about Iwo Jima in his twenty-minute tour than I did from any previous study of the event. Why? Because an active participant in the historical event brought it to life for me.

In the same way, the Holy Spirit was there when God dreamed our unique design into existence. Now the Holy Spirit is responsible for distributing those gifts to us in this life. What better guide for discovery could we have?

Listening

The Holy Spirit does communicate with us. For example, the Spirit specifically directed the apostle Paul away from certain regions and specifically toward other countries, using strong impressions and even a vision (Acts 16:6–10). Listening and watching for the Spirit's direction is critical, and noticing a small nudge can have amazing impact down the road if we heed it. Often we spend so much time working, talking, and doing that the busyness of life drowns out the whispers of the Holy Spirit.

Several years ago as a difficult season of my life was coming to an end, God used the opportunity to speak to me and prepare our family for the next season. I'd vocalized that I was ready no matter what the next step was, even packing our bags and moving overseas if that was God's calling.

Bill Hybels had just released a book called *The Power of a Whisper*. Although I'd not read the book, I was looking forward to hearing Bill speak at a conference. During the worship before Bill spoke, God moved powerfully and personally in my heart. I was literally brought to my knees in tears when a voice said to me, "Are you ready?" Without hesitation, I said, "Yes!"

But ready for what?

Bill came up to speak. He started to share about his new book and said, "I've found that the Holy Spirit often speaks to me in three-word fragments or short sentences." Wow. What an amazing and timely confirmation. Yes, the Spirit had my attention, and I was ready. So as I sat there listening to Bill, I asked God, "What do you want me to do?" The Holy Spirit then clearly said, "Write!"

I'd never written a book, and I didn't consider myself an author with anything particularly interesting to say. I wasn't a public speaker with a desire for a stage or microphone. I was and am actually cynical about leaders who feel so compelled to write books. So when the Spirit said, "Write!" I thought, "Okay, now maybe I am crazy and hearing things." Writing would be priority 999 on my to-do list of 1000. I confess it took time to get over my personal reluctance, but eventually clarity emerged in the form of this book.

For me, this book is a response to the voice of God through the Holy Spirit. My role of obedience has been simply to respond to the voice. The measure of success? Completing the work God gave to me. Obedience to the whisper is the only responsibility I carry. What God does with my obedience is all his.

Consider the rhythms of your life. Are you intentionally and deliberately taking time each day to listen for the whispers of the Holy Spirit? How often do you sit and reflect in stillness, listening for the Holy Spirit to speak?

What if we got into the habit of committing just five minutes each day to reflecting in silence, listening for the guidance of the Holy Spirit?

The Holy Spirit should become the whisper we hear like a shout.

Making It Personal

To embrace the truths of calling, I will continually strive to submit to the guidance and power of the Holy Spirit, trusting him to reveal the unique clues of my personal calling.

trusting
the Guide

Calling is discovered when we allow the one who designed us to guide us on the journey.

Calling moves us from reliance on our own power and strength to reliance on the wisdom, power, and leading of the Holy Spirit. We learn to listen and we can get better at this over time. Look for the ways God is leading you day to day and respond well!

Calling Foundations

Clarity of calling emerges when we learn to:

1. Trust deeply the author of our story.
2. Step forward in faith, even when we cannot see clearly.
3. Abandon the earthbound kingdom of me in order to gladly serve in the eternal kingdom of God.
4. Submit to the lordship of Jesus.
5. Embrace our mission to carry the fullness of Jesus to every corner of society.
6. Live in common with a healthy, local community of faith.
7. Take personal responsibility of the unique role Jesus gives us.
8. Trust the guidance and power of the Holy Spirit.

Visit www.personalcalling.org for supplemental resources.

CHAPTER 8

Discovering My
Unique Role

Yet you, LORD, are our Father.
We are the clay, you are the potter;
we are all the work of your hand.

ISAIAH 64:8

Several years ago, a single statement by a mentor changed
my trajectory. Bob Buford, author of *Halftime*, a book I
read during my own struggle with calling, approached me
about working together on several projects. I was considering
investing about 20 percent of my time in these projects when
Bob said, "I want you to function 100 percent in your sweet
spot in the work you do with me. I don't want you to do
anything that is not in your sweet spot."

In an instant, this simple statement sent shock waves
to my soul, expressing itself in three different, almost
simultaneous thoughts and emotions. First, Bob's comment
totally energized me. Every cell in my body cried out in
unison, "*Yes!* A role where I can function 100 percent in my
sweet spot."

That excitement quickly dissipated as a practical question
entered my head: "What would it look like to function

100 percent in my sweet spot?" I came face-to-face with the truth that I might not know what my sweet spot looked like if it hit me between the eyes. That wouldn't do.

As an engineer, I'm naturally conditioned to compare reality to possibility. In this case, the possibility of what could be—living within my sweet spot, designed by God uniquely for me—was not something I'd ever thought about. Accepting a position with the requirement that I function 100 percent in my sweet spot would require further work on my part to even know how I was doing.

As the reality of not understanding my own sweet spot set in, a third question filled my mind, further deflating the momentary excitement. "Why in the world am I getting so excited about spending only 20 percent of my time in my sweet spot? Why do I settle for such a low standard? Why am I satisfied with anything less than 100 percent of my time in the sweet spot of God's handiwork for me?"

Bob's simple comment put me on a journey of discovery. A journey into the mysterious land of calling. A journey I'm now convinced is part of who God made me to be. A journey I'm passionate about helping as many other people as possible take. This journey transforms our hearts and positions us as God's people to live the abundant life Jesus came to give.

This chapter provides the framework I've used in coaching others and in discovering and refining my own sweet spot of calling.

A Masterpiece with a Sweet Spot of Calling

Check out what David says about us being God's masterpiece:

> For you created my inmost being;
> you knit me together in my mother's womb.
> I praise you because I am fearfully and wonderfully made;
> your works are wonderful,
> I know that full well.

My frame was not hidden from you
  when I was made in the secret place,
  when I was woven together in the depths of the earth.
Your eyes saw my unformed body;
  all the days ordained for me were written in your book
  before one of them came to be.
How precious to me are your thoughts, God!
  How vast is the sum of them!
Were I to count them,
  they would outnumber the grains of sand—
  when I awake, I am still with you. (Psalm 139:13–18)

Let these words about God's handiwork in our lives sink in: We are fearfully and wonderfully made by the Creator of the universe. He envisioned our lives before the substance of our bodies was formed. David's words are deeply personal and reflect a potter who is lovingly shaping clay into a masterpiece. As his masterpieces, we see that we each have a sweet spot, a unique design, custom built to serve the Creator's purposes.

What Is a Sweet Spot?

Sometimes it's easier to understand a concept by starting with what it is not. About a year after purchasing new tires for my car, I began feeling a slight vibration through the steering wheel. Several months later the symptoms expanded to include an audible "thump, thump, thump." Within six months the vibration had gotten so bad that I began to worry about potential damage to other parts in the suspension system from the violent nature of the shaking.

After taking the car to a mechanic, I learned that the root cause of the problem was the tires being out of balance. Amazingly, the fix was to position a small weight in precisely the correct position on the wheel. The improper positioning of this four-ounce wheel weight was preventing a two-thousand-pound car from performing as it was designed.

Think of it. A wheel weight perfectly positioned produces a seemingly frictionless and smooth ride. In a similar way, perfect contact with a ball on the bat's sweet spot produces a home run, and a perfectly tuned and conditioned musical instrument played by a master resonates with a mysterious harmony to the soul.

In the physical world of God's creation there are thousands of sweet spots. Rooms have acoustic sweet spots, gun scopes have sweet spots, and musical instruments and sports equipment have sweet spots.

Calling is a sacred whisper from God. He calls us to himself and sends us to others. His handiwork in our unique design is part of that mysterious whisper. Like the pattern he established in his creation of the world, we are each uniquely and individually made with a sweet spot. These sweet spots are inseparable from our calling to and from God.

Characteristics of a Sweet Spot

When something functions within its sweet spot, the effort applied appears natural, smooth, and frictionless. You might say there is joy and a harmony in a sweet spot. Sweet spots are also multipliers of an input to produce an even greater output. They naturally turn one unit of effort into 100 units of result. Fruitfulness results from a properly functioning sweet spot.

So how does a sweet spot function? Every sweet spot in nature involves a design, a purpose, and a position. We can always ask, "Is it positioned correctly, doing what it's designed to do, and producing the results intended by its creator?"

This begs the question: Are you positioned correctly, doing what you are divinely designed to do, and producing the fruit intended by your Creator? Are you in his sweet spot for your life?

Three Questions of Purpose

Recall from chapter 3 that the consequence of sin and separation from God produces three natural questions in our lives. These are the questions you were already asking before you picked up this book, and they are the reason you're investigating the nature of calling. These three questions will help us to apply the truth of our sweet spot to real life.

1. Who am I created to BE? (a design or identity question)
2. What am I created to DO? (a purpose or mission question)
3. Where am I created to GO? (a compatibility or position question)

It's no accident that these three universally asked questions line up perfectly with the three elements of a sweet spot (i.e., every sweet spot has a design, a purpose, and a position). The answers to these BE-DO-GO questions represent our unique sweet spot of calling. The longing of our heart to respond to and live on the right side of our calling screams out to us through these questions, questions that reflect the natural elements of our sweet spot.

The Sweet Spot of Calling

The Creator of the universe uniquely designed me before I was born for specific good works that he wants me to accomplish. Remember that this promise is for every believer and not just a few heroes of the faith. Let the weight of this truth resonate deeply. God has a destiny for us, crafted by him and worked into the very fabric of creation. It is a perfectly fitted plan, forming a sweet spot of who we are.

> For we are God's handiwork, created in Christ Jesus to do good works, which God prepared in advance for us to do. (Ephesians 2:10)

Just as nature shows us that every sweet spot exhibits (1) a design, (2) a purpose, and (3) a positioning, we see these elements in Ephesians 2:10:

Design: We are created by his workmanship. He gives each of us a custom design that helps uniquely shape our sweet spot. We are a masterpiece of his hands, and because we are created in his image, our unique design is a reflection of him to the world. We are called to be stewards of what he's uniquely given each of us. Who we are created to BE is about our unique identity.

Purpose: We are created for unique good works prepared and planned by God. We yield and surrender to his purposes. He is the potter and we are the clay. Our good works, prepared by God, are part of his larger epic plans for redeeming human-kind. Just as our lives are like puzzles with many pieces, our lives are one piece of God's larger purpose. What we were made to DO is about our unique mission.

Positioning: God intends for us to use our unique design in the specific good works he's prepared for each of us. The King James Version of Ephesians 2:10 says, "For we are his workmanship, created in Christ Jesus unto good works, which God hath before ordained that we should walk in them." "That we should walk in them" is a call to action in specific places. Where we are to GO is about our unique position.

This framework of sweet spot represents the integration of issues of our heart, our head, and our hands. At its core, our sweet spot is about who we are in Christ Jesus. Our growth and maturity in being and becoming are to overflow and shape our doing and accomplishing.

Our sweet spot of calling is defined by the intersection of our unique identity, the good works he calls us to accomplish, and the place we are called to do it.

Primary and Secondary Calling

Calling is God's sacred whisper that draws us into his mission on earth and plans for eternity. This whisper draws us to have the fullness of Jesus in us and to channel it through us to others. You might say there are two parts: a general calling and a unique calling, or what some theologians have called a primary calling and a secondary calling.

Cotton Mather, the American colonial historian, theologian, and author who cofounded Yale University, described two parts of calling. He referred to the first as a "general calling" to be a witness to the truth of Jesus in our lives. This general calling applies to all Christians, everywhere, all the time. This general calling unites the body of Christ in a shared response to God's plans. Other theologians have referred to this general calling as our "primary calling."

Our general or primary calling is to be disciples who make disciples where we are! This element of calling is the fullness of Jesus flowing in us and through us to others. When the Bible refers to "calling" it is most often this primary or general calling.

However, Mather also identified a second element he referred to as "personal" or "unique calling." Personal calling represents the unique, divine equipping God gives each believer to help carry the fullness of Jesus to the world. In Mather's words, this personal calling finds its context in a "certain particular employment, by which [a person's] usefulness in his neighborhood is distinguished." Other theologians have referred to this personal or unique calling as our "secondary calling."

As discussed previously, the church's mission is to be the fullness of Jesus everywhere and in every way. That starts with the fullness of Jesus in us, and then extends to his fullness through us and to others (primary or general calling). We each have a personal responsibility, as part of the larger church family, to be disciples (the fullness of Jesus in us) who make disciples (the fullness of Jesus through us), in the mission field where we are.

We simultaneously have the responsibility to use our unique giftedness, given by Jesus himself, to do good works where we can be most effective in taking the fullness of Jesus into every nook and cranny of society. Our secondary or unique personal calling equips us to play a unique part in accomplishing God's mission in our community.

In *Courage and Calling*, Gordon Smith writes, "First, there is the call to be a Christian.... Second, for each individual there is a specific call—a defining purpose or mission, a reason for being. Every individual is called of God to respond through service in the world. Each person has a unique calling in this second sense. We cannot understand this second meaning of call except in the light of the first."[1]

You may be tempted to say, "I understand the general calling to be a disciple who makes disciples. I want to focus on my unique personal calling. That's where I'm confused." Avoid that trap. The two must function in tandem.

Cotton Mather gives us a picture ("model") for how the two elements of calling should integrate. He says: "A Christian at his two callings is a man in a boat rowing. If he mind but one of his callings, be it which it will, he pulls the oar, but on one side of the boat, and will make but a poor dispatch to the shore of eternal blessedness. It is not only necessary that a Christian should follow his general calling, it is of necessity that he follow his personal calling, too."[2]

Mather highlights the consequence of only putting one oar in the water (or engaging one of the two dimensions of calling). We will move in circles, never accomplishing the mission we were made for.

Bob Buford highlights this with two questions he says we will all face someday before Jesus.

First, how did you respond to who Jesus said he was? Did you respond and surrender to his lordship, living your life in submission to him? This is our primary or general calling at its heart.

Second, what did you do with what he uniquely gave you to work with? How did you respond to the unique abilities and design he gave you and the good works he called you to? This is our secondary or unique personal calling.

Notice how the answer to the second question only finds true meaning and significance when it grows out of our answer to the first question. Primary and secondary calling must function in tandem.

A Framework for Calling

Our unique design or identity (our BE) informs our mission (our DO), which in turn informs our mission field (our GO). Our design or identity is a question of "who." Our mission or purpose is a question of "what." And our mission field or position is a question of "where." The model might look something like this:

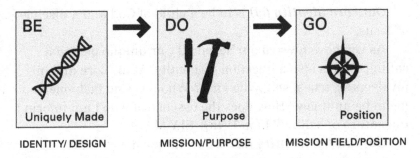

IDENTITY/ DESIGN   MISSION/PURPOSE   MISSION FIELD/POSITION

A good model deconstructs the Be-Do-Go sweet spot into simple parts, allowing us to isolate and study the characteristics of each part. The parts include our identity (BE), our mission (DO), and our position (GO).

Instead of trying to figure out the entire picture at once, we can focus on the individual parts and then integrate our learning into a more comprehensive understanding of our calling. You might say that we can put each element under a microscope for study. As we gain increasing clarity on the parts, we then seek to integrate them into a better understanding of how the parts work together.

In applying our BE-DO-GO framework to both primary and secondary calling, as discussed above, we end up with six core elements in our model (three for primary calling and three for secondary). Let's take a deeper look at these six elements, looking at the integration of both primary and secondary calling.

MY IDENTITY: WHO AM I CREATED TO BE?

All Christians are called to be children of God and to be disciples of Jesus. Unlike other titles and roles such as husband, wife, boss, engineer, and coach that are temporary, the role of child of God is permanent and transcends this life into eternity. We are called to be healthy, functioning children in God's family. The BE element of primary or general calling shared by all Christians is to BE DISCIPLES. In being disciples of Jesus, we seek first to have his fullness in us and to become more like him.

Our *core identity (cI)* is to be a child of God and a disciple of Jesus.

As we move toward our secondary or unique personal calling, this is also a question of identity. At my core and in my deepest, truest self, who am I? Who has God fashioned me to be uniquely? How does the essence of who I am inform the nature of calling? I am UNIQUELY MADE.

Our *unique identity (uI)* is our unique design that distinguishes us from God's other children.

MY MISSION: WHAT AM I CREATED TO DO?

At its heart, this is a question of mission or purpose. In universal terms, our answer is clear.

All Christians are called to make disciples. We are to be witnesses of his love that others may be drawn to him and become disciples. In our primary or general calling, we are to MAKE DISCIPLES.

Our *core mission (cM)* is to make disciples.

We are to be fully surrendered to Jesus and his commands and to be love in action. The overflow of Jesus' love for us prompts us to love other people through our good works and deeds. But what specific good works should I focus on? That's the right question. Answering it individually will be part of the journey, which will continue far beyond the reading of this book. In our secondary or unique personal calling we are to do unique GOOD WORKS AND DEEDS.

Our *unique mission (uM)* is the unique purpose assigned to us by God that produces unique good works and deeds in our lives.

MY POSITION: WHERE AM I CREATED TO GO?

Where am I created to go? It's a question about positioning.

We are to be disciples and make disciples wherever we are and in whatever we are doing. We are to be the love of Jesus everywhere we go with intentionality and urgency. Our general or primary calling shared with all Christians, everywhere, at all times is to be disciples who make disciples WHEREVER WE ARE.

Our *core position (cP)* is the opportunities right where we are.

In our restlessness to "go," we must first look at our stewardship of what's been given to us where we are. We need to be a disciple who makes disciples here and now. There is no elusive "tomorrow" in some yet-to-be-determined foreign land. Faithfulness to our calling begins with being a good steward of the opportunities every day where we are.

He might call you to radically change your lifestyle or your expected level of comfort for the sake of where he is leading you. And the destination may be right where you are, or it might not be completely clear yet. The amazing thing is that not only is he preparing you internally to fit his plan, he is also working out the external place you will serve as well.

Our secondary or unique personal calling prompts us not just to serve where we are, but to be willing to reposition ourselves to go WHERE WE CAN BE MOST EFFECTIVE.

Our *unique position (uP)* is the context where we can be most effective.

In pulling these elements of primary and secondary calling together into a single framework, we get the following:

My primary or general calling	=	My Core Identity (cI)	+	My Core Mission (cM)	+	My Core Position (cP)
My secondary or unique personal calling	=	My Unique Identity (uI)	+	My Unique Mission (uM)	+	My Unique Position (uP)

	BE	DO	GO
	My Core Identity (cI)	*My Core Mission (cM)*	*My Core Position (cP)*
Primary or General Calling	Be a disciple of Jesus	who makes disciples	where I am!
	BE **Uniquely Made** IDENTITY/ DESIGN	**DO** Purpose MISSION/PURPOSE	**GO** Position MISSION FIELD/ POSITION
Secondary or Unique Personal Calling	I am uniquely made	to do good works and deeds	where I can be most effective!
	My Unique Identity (uI)	*My Unique Mission (uM)*	*My Unique Position (uP)*

We can treat each of these six elements as lenses that give insight into who we are. Our job ahead is to look more deeply at each of these six lenses.

Applying Lenses

A lens provides insight and clarity, bringing the characteristics of whatever is studied more fully into focus. Within each lens are "clues" or "traits" that give insights into who we are. The more clues or traits we can see, the better the clarity of the picture.

Generically, the graphic below represents one of our six lenses. At the center of each lens is "me," as if I'm looking in the mirror or as if a lens is projecting a truth about me and my unique design onto a wall. Each of the lines projecting from the center is a space to insert words (or word phrases) that describe me. The lens simply serves as a tool to help me collect an increasing number of traits that help clarify this particular element of calling.

Each line extending from the center is a characteristic that brings more clarity to what is in the center of the lens. Think of each line as a clue to be discovered and understood. The more clues you discern, the better your clarity. The clues emerge throughout our lives, ready for discovery.

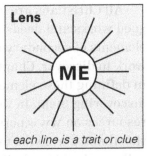

each line is a trait or clue

In coming chapters we will apply these lenses to gain clarity on each of the six elements of calling.

Looking Ahead . . .

We find ourselves back at the question sparked by Bob Buford at the beginning of this chapter: What would it take to live 100 percent in our sweet spot? Answer: It takes work. We must go through the discipline and hard work of discovering who we are created to be in Christ Jesus.

You probably picked up this book to gain more clarity on your secondary or unique personal calling. Have patience. A core truth of sweet spot is that our unique calling and good works can only find purpose and meaning within the context of our primary and general calling to be and make disciples everywhere we go. The good news is that a lot of the picture is already filled in!

For example, Jesus gives us the general direction of our primary or general calling that applies to all Christians, everywhere, all the time. We are called to be disciples (core identity—cI) who make disciples (core mission—cM) where they are (core position—cP). Our job is to find the unique contextualization of these elements in our lives and in the sphere of the relationships we find ourselves in.

In chapters 9–11 and in the supporting resources on www.personalcalling.org, we use the following shorthand acronyms to refer to these three elements of primary calling: cI, cM, and cP.

All Christians are also uniquely made to do specific good works and deeds where they can be most effective. The elements of secondary or unique calling require time and work to discover. Chapters 12–14 will go into greater detail in defining these elements and providing a roadmap for discovering them. In these chapters and in the supporting resources on www.personalcalling.org, we use the following shorthand acronyms to refer to the elements of secondary calling: uI, uM, and uP.

In the coming chapters, we will look more deeply at each of the six elements (cI, cM, cP, uI, uM, and uP). The story God has already written in your life reveals hundreds of clues or traits ready for you to bring into sharper focus with each of the six elements. The people in your life, including your spouse, children, parents, friends, and coworkers can add hundreds more clues. Various tests and self-assessments will be introduced to provide even more detail.

You will begin to apply the process of collecting and aggregating clues and traits about your calling. Along the way we will discuss the process of integrating and condensing the words into simple and memorable elements that define your call. This calling model can continue to be used and refined over your entire lifetime. Our goal throughout the rest of this book is to establish a discipline and some momentum in applying this model, hoping that it becomes a lifestyle.

Making It Personal

To embrace the truths of calling, I will be a disciple of Jesus seeking to become more filled with his fullness, allowing that fullness to overflow to others as I seek to make disciples wherever I am. I will be a good steward of God's unique identity and mission in my life, wherever I can be most effective.

discovering
My Unique Role

Our primary or general calling is discovered in being disciples of Jesus (the fullness of Jesus in us) who make disciples (the fullness of Jesus through us) where we are. This is true of all Christians, everywhere, at all times.

Our secondary or unique calling is discovered where God's unique design in our lives overflows to specific good works and deeds wherever we can be most effective.

Calling moves us from being imperfect stewards of our unique gifting to being who we were created to be and doing what we were created to do. That shift is an incredibly exciting transition.

Calling equips us to be fully devoted disciples of Jesus.

Calling Foundations

Clarity of calling emerges when we learn to:

1. Trust deeply the author of our story.

2. Step forward in faith, even when we cannot see clearly.

3. Abandon the earthbound kingdom of me in order to gladly serve in the eternal kingdom of God.

4. Submit to the lordship of Jesus.

5. Embrace our mission to carry the fullness of Jesus to every corner of society.

6. Live in common with a healthy, local community of faith.

7. Take personal responsibility of the unique role Jesus gives us.

8. Trust the guidance and power of the Holy Spirit.

9. Follow our general calling to be disciples of Jesus who make disciples where we are.Core Identity (cI) + Core Mission (cM) + Core Position (cP)

10. Fulfill our unique personal calling to play our role in God's mission where we can be most effective.Unique Identity (uI) + Unique Mission (uM) + Unique Position (uP)

Visit www.personalcalling.org for supplemental resources.

PART TWO

Discovering Your Calling

CHAPTER 9

Being a Disciple: My Core Identity

"Come, follow me!" Jesus said.

MATTHEW 4:19

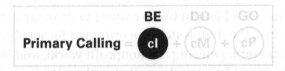

Primary calling. Who am I made to BE? What is my core identity (cI)?

Calling is found in the work of God in us, the act of truly being a disciple. In this chapter we take a deeper look at the BE element of our primary calling: our core identity (cI). Who are we called to be?

The Depth of Calling

My conversion at age twenty-four was genuine and transformative. But in retrospect, like the majority of Christians in the West, my response was more to "come and see" than to "come follow me." I gained access to eternal life but was missing out on the abundant life Jesus promises those who wholeheartedly follow him.

You see, abundant living comes through surrendering and focusing on the active pursuit of becoming. Jesus cares more about the condition of our hearts, our pursuit of holiness, and our *becoming* more like him than he does about our *doing* more for him. The "good life" in human terms is about me and building my kingship. The abundant life is about Jesus, becoming more like him, and his fullness in us overflowing to others.

It was many years after my initial conversion that God grabbed hold of me to "come and follow" in a much deeper way. The wrestling match was not about believing who Jesus was. Instead it was about where I would position that belief in my life. Would I more fully surrender and put him at the center where my relationship with him impacted everything else in my life, or would I leave him at the fringes where I could dial him up when needed during the difficulties of life?

For two years I fought God's calling to drop my nets and move into the divine steps he ordained for me. It meant changing careers, entering the nonprofit world, and leaving an organization I loved and excelled within. While it didn't result in the threat of persecution or death, it did require a heart makeover and steps of faith away from the security and comforts I'd grown accustomed to.

I confess these were years of trying to make the balance sheet add up. I'd take out a piece of paper and make two columns. On the left was life as it had been and was on track to be. Promotions, positions, influence, increasing salary, retirement plans, health plans, private schools, vacations, and a retirement date. All the worldly safety and security a person needs.

On the right side was life as it would be in pursuit of God's plans for me. Candidly, that column fell short of the list on the other side. Additionally, nearly every item on the right side was filled with uncertainty, risk, and discomfort.

No matter what time or day I went through the motions of this exercise, the results came out the same. I did this exercise at least fifteen times hoping for a different outcome. I'm a relatively sane person, so why did I keep doing the same thing over and over again hoping for a different outcome? In retrospect, discontent was pounding inside of me with increasing intensity.

God had something he wanted to do in my heart to prepare me for the journey ahead. The hesitation in my heart to say "yes" was related to God's desire for me to put my balance sheet to death. That piece of paper became the idol that God needed to destroy. That piece of paper, and the heart problems that penned the words on it, were shackles holding me back from experiencing abundant life.

Our idols have a unique and profound foothold on each of us. Their roots go deep. Only through heart transformation can we break their grip. I came to realize that money was at the core of my struggle. God spent two years helping me put to death the false security represented in money. Years later I see the wisdom in God's patience with me and in dealing with these underlying heart issues. Unsacrificed idols will weaken or ultimately sabotage the adventure God has for us.

Like the rich young man asking Jesus what was needed to receive eternal life, I got a similar answer. Jesus looked at him and loved him and said, "One thing you lack. Go, sell everything you have and give to the poor, and you will have treasure in heaven. Then come, follow me" (Mark 10:21). I needed to trust God more than I trusted financial security. Our idols may be different, but the call to surrender them is the same. Surrender is expected in following Jesus.

Putting First Things First

Being a disciple and follower of Jesus is the first and most important dimension of calling. Surrendering to his lordship and putting his ways at the center of all of life is the core foundation that becomes a supporting pillar for all the other dimensions of calling. You might say it makes everything else possible.

As we've said already, this "yes" to Jesus is more than believing Jesus is who he says. It's submitting to his lordship and putting him at the center of everything. It's a wholehearted commitment to following him and becoming more like him. It's a pursuit of holiness that brings us into increasing oneness with God the Father and Jesus his Son. Holiness and idols can't coexist.

I will not sugarcoat the discomfort during that season when my wife, Anna, and I surrendered the good life we'd been living for the better one God designed for us to discover. It was not easy. But amidst those scary days was a peace that surpassed understanding. A calm that could only come from God and that made no sense given the magnitude and absurdity of our decision. A peace rooted in knowing that to do anything else would be willful disobedience, regardless of the circumstances.

The right side of my balance sheet finally won out when I embraced the scorecard of eternity in exchange for the worldly scorecard that was so deeply embedded in the kingship of me. You see, God wants to get us to a place of obedience where the circumstances of life and potential consequences of our steps to follow him don't hinder us. A place where we stop dwelling on worldly concerns of what might be versus the keen awareness of who we are in Christ Jesus. When we sincerely take steps of obedience, we've taken hold of the first and vital element of calling: Being a disciple who moves from "come and see" to "follow me."

The Step of Yes

Consider Deborah, answering God's call to lead Israel in troubled times during an age when female leadership was all but unheard of. Her "yes" came with God's anointing and in direct opposition to the role that culture would define for her. Calling isn't always popular or "normal"; sometimes it will involve something new and completely unexpected.

Or think about Peter, Noah, Nehemiah, Elisha, Daniel,

or any of the great captains and heroes of the faith. We don't often learn about their initial conversions. Instead we generally pick up their story in midstride with a vibrant relationship with God already present. The subsequent surrender to calling for all of these leaders, and for us, may be more costly or difficult than our initial entry into faith.

The invitation to "come and see" (John 1:39) that the disciples first heard from Jesus was much safer than the "come and follow me" they responded to as they journeyed with him, even to his death. Seen from the outside, from a worldly and natural perspective, a disciple's "yes" to Jesus' second invitation seems epic and in some ways even alarming.

Take Peter, for instance. When Jesus called him to be a disciple, Peter's "yes" was resounding. But did he really know what he was saying yes to? He likely wanted a mission. He wanted clarity. He wanted action. Like us, he wanted to experience significance in doing something bigger than himself, something more than the day-to-day struggle to make a living. But before Jesus could use Peter, he needed the full surrender of Peter's heart.

To fully become a disciple of Jesus, we must respond with a heartfelt yes to Jesus' call. As we put Jesus at the center of our identity, other elements of our calling will come into focus.

The challenge is to acknowledge honestly where you are relative to the surrender Jesus requires. Do you need to move from "come and see" to "come follow me"? Are you ready to say, "Yes"?

Our Wholehearted Devotion

The author of the book of Hebrews deals directly with our need to throw off anything that weighs us down and keeps us from becoming more like Jesus. He says: "Therefore, since we are surrounded by such a great cloud of witnesses, let us throw off everything that hinders and the sin that so easily entangles. And let us run with perseverance the race marked out for us, fixing our eyes on Jesus, the pioneer and perfecter of faith" (Hebrews 12:1–2).

The author's metaphor of a race is perfect. The pursuit of holiness is represented by a race toward Jesus. Our eyes are to be focused on him at the finish line. The race is intended to make us more like him as we pursue him and get closer to him.

To win races, athletes must be disciplined in their training. Diet and exercise become top priorities and integrated into their everyday lifestyle. I recently talked with a young man seeking to enter the professional ranks of mixed martial arts fighting. He had been training for two years, going to the gym twice a day, seven days a week. In preparing for his first fight, he quit his job and spent four full months dedicated to his preparations. That is devotion.

I recently restored an older, expensive guitar. My son bought the damaged heap of wood to repair, but I took on the project as a hobby and became devoted to bringing it back to life. The smashed and damaged top of this expensive guitar made it essentially worthless when I started.

In talking with the manufacturer of the guitar, I learned that the cost of repair was greater than its value. The challenge had been defined. After all, driven leaders love the thrill and pursuit of victory. No heap of smashed wood was going to stop this budding, amateur guitar repairman. Despite my inexperience, I had one thing going for me: devotion to a cause.

I found closely matched replacement wood from a forestry company in Oregon and learned the process of hand repairing the vintage instrument. I spent hundreds of hours painstakingly repairing and bringing that guitar back to life. By the time I finished, my hourly wage based on the resale value of the restored guitar was less than $2 per hour.

Far more important and relevant than the money was how my devotion to the cause produced a true love for the instrument. As the guitar neared completion, my son became excited at the prospect of selling the guitar and the resulting "profits." Before I could respond my wife declared, "No. Your dad has invested too much time and energy in that guitar to ever sell it."

Because of my affection and devotion, that guitar got some of the best of my time, talent, and treasure. Everything we own also owns a part of us. The good, the bad, and the ugly. Let that sink in. We have a choice in what will own the best of us. It's a choice we make every day, day after day. Anything that becomes an object of greater wholehearted devotion than Jesus becomes an idol.

When we fully and wholeheartedly devote ourselves to Jesus, we can do extraordinary things. As long as our devotion is focused on Jesus, we see our holiness accelerate. Holiness isn't about "thou shalt not." Instead, it's about love. Holiness is spurred on by our full, wholehearted devotion to Christ!

In this pursuit, we must keep our eyes and affection fixed on Jesus. It's a daily battle requiring daily commitment. We must run to and for him, seeking to become more like him, continually assessing whether the things of the world are becoming the primary objects of our affection rather than Jesus. We must be like the mixed martial arts fighter fixed on the pursuit of a goal that influences our lifestyle 24/7.

The Sweetness of Being

My friend Ed Bahler had a near-death experience that brought him face-to-face with the kind of surrender God wants of us. Within weeks of Christmas celebrations with his children and grandchildren, Ed learned that he had pancreatic cancer. This is a deadly form of cancer with only 20 percent of people living one year and only 4 percent living five years. Within forty-eight hours the doctor was performing surgery, and Ed's world was turned upside down.

As Ed and I discussed this book on calling and the importance of surrender, Ed described what happened to him during those forty-eight hours between diagnosis and surgery. Suddenly nothing on the left side of his balance sheet made any difference at all. Instead, his world collapsed to the reality of death and his limited time on earth. With the ultimate surrender of his physical life looming, issues of identity in Christ naturally emerged.

Ed now describes the "sweetness" of those days where his primary focus was on experiencing Jesus and seeking to have his last days be a witness, a beautiful testimony and blessing to his family and friends. Isn't that the picture of what God wants from us as we walk into the good works and life he has planned for us? He desires to bring us to a place where our identity in Christ and our obedience to him trumps anything on the left side of our balance sheet.

Regardless of our circumstances or the consequences, we experience God's "sweetness" as we reflect his glory to the world around us. Our stories, like Ed's reflection of Jesus to his family, are intended to reflect God's glory to the world.

As you wrestle with surrender, understand the difference between peace and comfort. The surrender to the journey of calling is most certainly filled with discomfort. By its very nature, surrender is uncomfortable. However, God's peace accompanies surrender, making the right column of our balance sheet weightier than the left. This peace is a tangible manifestation of God's grace in our lives. Add it to your balance sheet as you wrestle with surrendering to the more abundant life God has in store for you.

Weigh the cost and consider the benefits as you look to move beyond a "come and see" posture to a "come follow me" life.

Then give your entire heart to the *yes*. Be a disciple!

Application: The Lens of Core Identity (cI)

Earlier, we introduced the idea of "lenses" for each of the six dimensions of calling. The first lens is designed to help us identify specific characteristics of our core identity (cI). We are created to BE children of God and disciples of Jesus. Our core identity is found in becoming more like Jesus.

This first lens is designed to produce a clear picture of the characteristics of fullness Jesus calls us to. How would we describe someone who has the fullness of Jesus in them? The New Testament highlights over one hundred such characteristics. Our role is to make these characteristics personal in our lives.

Here is a suggested exercise to support the first lens of calling. Visit www.personalcalling.org to see an example of this exercise in action:

Step 1: Do a survey of one of the Gospels (Matthew, Mark, Luke, or John). You don't have to read every word. Look for specific actions and attributes of Jesus that reflect who he is. Actions and attributes like "He went aside to pray" or "Jesus had compassion on them." Make a list of these characteristics. Turn descriptions from the Gospel narrative into truths about Jesus' character. Be concise. There will be many duplicates and different ways of describing the same characteristic. Don't worry about details. Simply write down all the characteristics you can find. A repeated characteristic simply means it is particularly important.

Step 2: Condense the list into a more concise and distinct set of characteristics without duplicates. Look for words and phrases that mean the same thing. Use words and phrases that are memorable or personally significant for you.

Step 3: Seek to further condense the list into about 5–7 groupings, each with a heading. For example, several

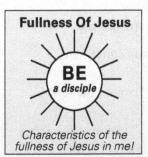
Characteristics of the fullness of Jesus in me!

characteristics from step 2 may fit under the heading "gentleness" or "self-control" or "compassion" or "generosity." The intent is to develop a list of core characteristics that provide a good picture of what it looks like for the fullness of Jesus to be in someone. Add the list of groupings to the "lens" shown on the previous page. The lines extending out from the center represent the characteristics of the fullness of Jesus in the life of a fully devoted follower. The number of lines is arbitrary and based on the number of characteristics you come up with.

Step 4: Using the words that are most meaningful from step 3, seek to personalize a core identity statement. Start with the statement "my core identity (cI) is to be a disciple of Jesus who . . ." Next, build onto the end of this statement using words from step 3 that are personally meaningful to you and modify your core identity statement to make it more personal.

Personal Questions and Assessment

This first lens gives us a picture of what the fullness of Jesus looks like as it continues to mature in the life of one who has moved from "come and see" to "follow me." Remember, our "yes" is simply the surrender that positions us for heart transformation and for becoming more like Jesus. The characteristics will develop over time as our hearts are transformed. Our relationship with Jesus as his disciples makes the transformation possible.

If you've not yet taken that step of full surrender to "follow me," let that decision be the primary focus of your pursuit in discerning your unique calling. As discussed in the last chapter, the other five elements of calling have limited usefulness in the absence of the wholehearted "yes" required of this first element.

Spend some time reflecting on these questions:

- What aspects of saying "yes" to Jesus convict or challenge you?
- Where are you on the spectrum of "come and see" versus "come follow me"?
- In what ways is the "kingship of me" keeping you from more fully surrendering to the lordship of Jesus?

- What idols are preventing Jesus from being at the center of your life?
- What behaviors need to change for you to become more like Jesus (based on a personal assessment of the characteristics you discovered in the exercise above)?
- What barriers stand in the way of your becoming more like Jesus?
- What are your biggest fears and uncertainties in saying "yes"?
- What specifically needs to happen now, without delay, regardless of where you are on the spectrum?

Calling is found in our core identity (cI) overflowing into action. In the following chapter we take a deeper look at the DO element of primary or general calling, our core mission (cM). What are we called to DO with what's been given to us?

Visit www.personalcalling.org for supplemental resources.

CHAPTER 10

Making Disciples: My Core Mission

With this in mind, we constantly pray for you,
that our God may make you worthy of his calling,
and that by his power he may bring to fruition your
every desire for goodness and your every deed
prompted by faith.

2 THESSALONIANS 1:11

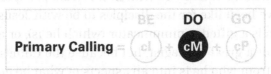

Primary calling. What am I made to DO? What is my core mission (cM)?

In recent years I've become friends with Dr. Robert Coleman, distinguished senior professor of discipleship and evangelism at Gordon Conwell Theological Seminary. It takes only a few minutes in his presence to know something is very different about him. My wife says he is the greatest gentleman she's ever met. When I picture Moses glowing after his encounter with God at the burning bush, I think of Dr. Coleman. He is anointed with the fullness of Jesus in a way that overflows to the world. His presence radiates the fullness of Jesus.

My friend Kennon Vaughn was mentored and discipled by Dr. Coleman. I asked him to describe how Dr. Coleman impacts him. Kennon says: "I've never met a guy who lives his life as worshipfully. Dr. Coleman models what it looks like to pray continually. He has one foot in glory, always thinking eternally. At times he will spontaneously burst out in laughter as he thinks about heaven. He has a renewed, transformed mind. It's incredibly inspiring. It's what I read in the Scriptures coming to life in bodily form. While most of us are caught up in the external worldly things of 'doing,' Dr. Coleman is focused on the 'being' of abiding in Christ and his fullness. Dr. Coleman models a lifestyle for me to aspire to and a target to shoot for. He inspires me to my knees. He inspires me to minister out of the overflow of my devotion to Christ as opposed to my own strength. He naturally inspires me to refocus my priorities on Jesus and to become more like him. Dr. Coleman is a disciple who makes disciples who makes disciples. I want to be like him!"

I'm also naturally drawn to and want to be like Dr. Coleman. I want to sit at his feet. To be with him is a snapshot of what it must have been like for the disciples to be with Jesus. Not because he is a gifted communicator (which he is), or a great visionary, or a great strategist, but because the fullness of Jesus overflows from who he is into all aspects of what he does in his life.

Disciples who make disciples the way God intends have something to offer that others want. This is why the first element of calling from chapter 9—having the fullness of Jesus in us—is so vitally important. It's not our unique giftedness that will change the world. It's the fullness of Jesus in us and through us that's the secret sauce.

Bill Hull, a mutual friend with Dr. Coleman, was looking through Dr. Coleman's severely worn Bible that is literally held together by tape. As Bill looked inside, the names of hundreds of men and women handwritten in the margins jumped off the pages. Bill asked, "Who are these people?" Dr. Coleman said, "Those are my boys. Hundreds of them now scattered around the world doing ministry and making disciples. Men and women I've discipled through the years who are now discipling others."

What's so special about Dr. Coleman's approach? Turn the clock back to the early 1960s. Dr. Coleman was a seminary professor pulling together a course on how Jesus did evangelism and made disciples. There were few comprehensive resources on the subject, so he turned directly to the Gospels to create his own.

Dr. Coleman asks, "How did Jesus do it?" Then he answers, "It's so simple. We just need to stop trying all the newest strategies and return to Jesus' way of doing it." At the core are a few simple, reproducible practices that any follower of Jesus can imitate and embrace: intentionality, relationships, teaching, modeling, practice, accountability, and reproduction.

Dr. Coleman turned what he'd learned into a book called *The Master Plan of Evangelism*. Since its publication in 1963 the book has been read by millions of people and has become the benchmark for understanding Jesus' method of disciple making. Rick Warren, founder of Saddleback Church and author of *The Purpose Driven Life*, read Dr. Coleman's book as a teenager and now says it was one of the foundational books that shaped his ministry. Billy Graham believed the secret of the book's success is Dr. Coleman's return to the Bible rather than fads and strategies to answer the simple question: What was the discipleship strategy of Jesus?

More important than his book, however, is that Dr. Coleman put what he learned into practice. Each year for over fifty years, he has recruited a small group of men and women to join him weekly in studying Jesus' life. But it's more than a Bible study. Dr. Coleman invests his life into these leaders as he comes alongside them. No secret or comprehensive strategies. He simply seeks to do with those young men and women what Jesus did with the disciples.

Discipleship is a lifestyle for Dr. Coleman. Ten to twelve leaders per year for over fifty years. Do the math. Step back and reflect on that impact and legacy. His secondary calling and giftedness is important, but far more profound is the fulfillment of his general calling to be a disciple who makes disciples. Those 500+ disciples he's personally invested in are now repeating for others what Dr. Coleman did for them. Their stories now find their context in all corners of the earth. More important is the amazing ripple effect of disciples making disciples who make disciples. Those leaders are now repeating around the world what they experienced with Dr. Coleman.

Dr. Coleman's personal calling as an evangelist teacher is important, but his impact only finds its context and meaning in supporting our general calling to make disciples.

Into Action

As Dr. Coleman demonstrates with his life, the fullness of Jesus *in me* is to overflow *through me* to others.

I love the words penned to Jewish Christians in the book of Hebrews. The author spends an entire chapter inspiring readers by reminding them of the heroes of the Jewish faith. "By faith Abraham . . . by faith Noah . . . by faith Moses . . ." In every case, the outcome of faith is action. They are united by their common faith, and their faith expresses itself in action. Paul sums it up by basically saying, "Therefore, since we've had faith in action modeled for us, we also should put our faith into action."

What does it look like to put the fullness of Jesus that is within us into action?

We are inspired by the legendary stories of faith we read about. If we are really honest, that is why we are fascinated by calling. We want to do great things that flow out of our unique gifting. However, when our worldly desire for impact gets out of sync with our eternal longings, we find ourselves pursuing significance with the wrong actions. We need our "doing" to overflow from our "being."

At the most fundamental level, the core mission (cM) that unifies us with all other followers of Jesus is this: We are to be disciples of Jesus (BE) who make disciples of others (DO). As we are discipled and become more fully surrendered followers of Jesus, his fullness overflows through us into the lives of others. Take away the foundational mission to "go and make disciples" and our faith is left to find its context in worldly pursuits and selfish ambitions.

We must start with a proper, biblical focus on making disciples as our general calling. Our unique personal calling will then come to life within that context. Be cautious of any motivation or foundation for action other than the shared mission of our general calling to be disciples who make disciples.

In this chapter we consider Jesus' method of discipleship and what it looks like for us to embrace our core mission to make biblical disciples.

Discipleship and Calling

Let's assume our personal calling is not randomly assigned by God but is uniquely given for us to bear fruit. Our gifting and calling are God's equipping for us to be fruitful by his measure of success.

Step back and consider how Jesus measures our fruit. Is his primary measure the disciple we become and the disciples we make as stewards of our general calling? Or is it the unique equipping we are given to do good works and deeds as a result of becoming his disciple and having his fullness overflow from us to others?

Both are important, but one exists to support the other. Our primary or general calling to be disciples who make disciples is messy and hard. Our secondary or unique personal calling is God's grace and unique equipping to help us be more effective in making disciples. This secondary calling must find its context within our general calling. Unfortunately, too many Christians never fully engage their more important general calling, opting instead to pursue a more glamorous unique personal calling as a way of discovering a more joy-filled and satisfying life.

Discipleship brings calling into focus and gives it meaning. Discipleship and calling are inseparable. Discipleship is the backbone of calling.

How then shall we live?

Keeping It Simple

Fortunately, Jesus' way of making disciples requires no special training or degrees or skill or strategy. Instead, it focuses squarely on how best to intentionally place the fullness of Jesus that is in me at the intersection of my relationships with others; and how best to position my life so that in my pursuit to be a better disciple I'm also making disciples.

We are to model what has been modeled to us. We are one link in a chain started by Jesus that makes its way from this temporary home on earth to our eternal home in heaven. It's a chain that has been passed down through the generations starting with the first twelve disciples of Jesus. We are all the spiritual children of the methods Jesus modeled for the twelve. The plan Jesus himself modeled for Peter and John and James and the other disciples is the same method that's been passed down to us for today. The approach works universally in all generations and in all contexts.

When Jesus commands that we "go and make disciples" (Matthew 28:19), he is adding us to the heroes of the faith listed in Hebrews. He is saying, "By your faith in me, and the fullness you experience as you abide in me, go and share that fullness with others that they also might become my disciples." The fruit of being a disciple is to make disciples. Focus on Jesus and experience his fullness. Live as Jesus lived. Love others. Invest in them and let the fullness of Jesus overflow into their lives. Some will become disciples.

Dr. Coleman told me, "I marvel at how impact multiplies, but the core plan of Jesus stays the same. We focus on our general calling to be disciples who make disciples, and we end up with reproducing leaders all over the world using their unique giftedness doing things and making an impact far greater than their teacher."

Two Sides of the Same Coin

Being a disciple and making disciples. Notice the synergy between the two. Being leads to making, but making requires the same core ingredients as being. As we make disciples, we become better disciples.

Good teachers agree that the process of teaching helps the teacher as much as the student. The same is true of disciple making. We can't experience the full measure of Jesus in us without making disciples. Dr. Coleman notes that he's a better disciple because of the disciples he's made. That just makes sense.

On one side of the discipleship coin is becoming a disciple and having the fullness of Jesus grow in us. On the other side is making disciples and sharing Jesus' fullness with others. In a discipling relationship, the fullness of Jesus never flows exclusively one way. When the fullness of Jesus is blossoming in others, it overflows to us, especially when we are the teacher. We can't choose just one side of the coin.

Our core identity (cI) overflows to shape our core mission (cM). Calling works that way.

Are you intentionally submitting to people in your life who disciple you? Do you have good role models like Dr. Coleman? If not, make that your first priority. Pursue them. Don't wait for them to find you. Find at least one person farther along in their faith journey who is willing to come alongside and disciple you. Put healthy, discipling relationships in your life. It's possibly the most important thing you can do in response to this book. Remember, the fullness of Jesus in you is the secret sauce to living a meaningful life in your calling. To disciple others, you also need to be discipled.

Questions to Wrestle With

What would be different if we wholeheartedly embraced measuring our primary legacy in this temporary life not by our personal accomplishments but rather by the impact of people we invested heavily in discipling each year? How would the world be different if just 1 percent of Christians embraced the practice Dr. Coleman has followed for the past fifty years? We could change the world and eternity in one generation!

What would that take? First, embracing our core identity (cI) with a newfound commitment to the lordship of Jesus. We need to move from cultural Christianity (come and see) to biblical Christianity (follow me). We must have the fullness of Jesus in us if that fullness is to be carried to the world. We must make the first element of our general calling to be disciples top priority in our lives.

Second, we must see our primary legacy on this earth through a new lens or scorecard. We must embrace the truth that our fruit will come not through our own accomplishments but rather through the people we disciple and invest in. We must embrace the core mission (cM) of God's primary calling on our lives to make disciples.

Third, we must be intentional to create space in our lives to invest in and disciple others. We must give the first fruits of our time and energy into investing in the people God is placing in our path.

As we do these three things, we pursue in tangible and practical ways both the great commandment (to love God and love people) and the great commission (to make disciples). Our secondary personal calling will find its context in supporting our efforts to invest into others.

Applying the Lens

As we've discussed, our core mission (cM) is the second element of our general calling. Like our core identity (cI) discussed in the last chapter, the good news is that we don't have to discern what our core mission is. Jesus gives it to us. We are to make disciples as an overflow of the fullness of Jesus in us.

At the center of this second lens is disciple making. What does it look like for disciple making to become a lifestyle for us? What would it look like for the fullness of Jesus to be so powerfully in us that we can't help but make disciples the way Jesus did? What are the specific behaviors and practices we must live out if disciple making is to become second nature?

Jesus came and modeled his methods for us. We need look no further than the Gospels to see how Jesus made disciples of his twelve students.

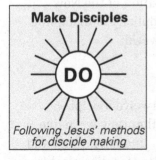

Extending from the center of the lens are lines that represent the practices and behaviors Jesus modeled. The rest of this section provides a brief overview of each of these elements.

Put yourself in the shoes of the apostle Peter or another of the other disciples who spent three years with Jesus. Step into the Gospel story and "live with Jesus" for three years. Read through one of the four Gospels of the Bible looking specifically at how Jesus interacted with and taught his disciples. As you do, think about your own life. How are these elements present or lacking? In looking at Jesus' way of making disciples with Dr. Coleman, we see the following characteristics.

JESUS

This may seem obvious, but he must be our starting and ending point. We are about Jesus. The fullness of him in us and through us brings life to everything else. Jesus is the subject of our affection and devotion. He is the author and perfecter of our faith and the One who gives meaning to our lives. We are to make disciples of him, not of ourselves or our idols. There is one Master and Lord.

INTENTIONALITY

Jesus was the most intentional and strategic person in history. He handpicked twelve followers and devoted three years of ministry to disciple them. He was not random. While he spoke to large crowds, his focus was still heavily on the development of the twelve disciples even in those settings. He could have chosen a pathway to speak to millions of people through large, stadium-like events. He could have used the power and worldly kingdom of Rome to shape future generations. He showed God's power through miracles and could have focused on revivals and healings. But the foundation of the New Testament church was based on the simplicity of discipling twelve followers to forever change the world.

RELATIONSHIP

Jesus lived in close proximity with the twelve disciples. Their lives were so deeply intertwined that they were like family. Relationships take commitment, intensity, time, and proximity. Relationships are the incubator for discipleship and the transformation that accompanies it. Dr. Coleman's yearly recruiting of his disciples resulted in a much different context for discipleship than that of teaching in a classroom. It's through relationships that our lives intertwine, trust is built, and we gain permission to speak into each other's lives.

TEACHING

Jesus said, "Go and make disciples of all nations . . . teaching them to obey everything I have commanded you" (Matthew

28:19–20). Jesus ties his teaching to discipleship. His teaching establishes the standard by which we are to live. His teaching helps his followers answer the most basic question, "As a disciple of Jesus, how should I live?"

So what is our authoritative standard? Obviously Jesus' words as reflected in the Gospels are vitally important. But the Bible did not exist when Jesus gave this command. He relied on those listening to his commands to pass them along in their own teaching and writing. We can trust that the truths given throughout the New Testament represent Jesus' teaching. We can and should take what we know of Jesus, his character, and his teachings and make deductions about "what would Jesus do" in our unique situations. In other words, in addition to teaching the verbatim words and commands of Jesus, we must teach people to think the way Jesus thought and to see the world the way he did.

Finally, teaching is a continuous, 24/7 lifestyle, not just a short, infrequent task. Jesus used every opportunity to teach his disciples. He taught while they walked, while they ate, and while they rode in boats. He even taught through his prayers.

MODELING

Jesus demonstrated for his disciples the things he asked them to do. The credibility of a leader and trust in any relationship is most dependent on living what we say and teach. In interviewing several of Dr. Coleman's disciples I consistently heard them say, "I want to live the way Dr. Coleman lives!"

EXERCISING/PRACTICING OUR FAITH

Jesus did not simply teach and model his commands; he also sent his disciples out to practice them. He then spent time debriefing their experiences and helping them become more effective. Real-life application has a way of sharpening and establishing our practices and behaviors like nothing else.

ACCOUNTABILITY

Jesus never failed to confront or even scold his disciples when they needed it. When Jesus told Peter, "Get behind me, Satan" (Matthew 16:23), he was being about as harsh as you can get. Jesus' disciples needed to know when their behavior and thinking were not consistent with his. The same is true for us and the people we disciple.

REPRODUCTION

Why did Jesus spend three years with twelve disciples? So the ripple of their multiplication would change the world. That ripple is embedded in the DNA of Jesus' method of discipleship. The fruit of discipleship is multiplication.

Again, we don't need a degree or special training in discipleship to jump in. Jesus' methods are very basic and reproducible.

Getting Intentional

My core mission (cM) within my primary calling is to make disciples, yet most Christians have never intentionally made disciples. Before moving into the next chapter, wrestle with the three questions below and reflect on changes you need to make to more fully embrace and live out this core mission (cM) to make disciples.

1. As a disciple of Jesus, how then should I live?
2. Are the elements Jesus used for making disciples present or lacking in my life?
3. What specific behaviors and practices must I live out for disciple making to become natural and organic?

Use the lens in this chapter to create and customize your own strategy, based on Jesus' way, for making disciples. Fill in the key elements that will form the foundation for your approach to making disciples. Seek to contextualize in a way that gives you a framework to work from for the rest of your life.

Your mission field may change through the years, but your basic approach and lifestyle for making disciples can remain the same.

The next logical question is: Where and with whom do we start?

Visit www.personalcalling.org for supplemental resources.

CHAPTER 11

Where I Am: My Core Position

Well done, good and faithful servant! You
have been faithful with a few things; I will put you
in charge of many things. Come and share your
master's happiness!

MATTHEW 25:21

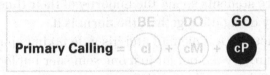

Primary calling. Where am I made to GO? Where is my core position (cP)?

In the last chapter we saw the impact of Dr. Robert Coleman being a disciple who makes disciples where he is. For over fifty years he has consistently and patiently made disciples in the context of intentional relationships. His disciples are now scattered all over the world, making disciples for Jesus where they are.

Years ago, Dr. Coleman and his wife, Marietta, entered a new season of life. Their children had left home and their net income was higher; they had also climbed the ladder of success within the college professor ranks of prestige and stature. They could have retired, moved into a beautiful house, hosted gala affairs, and coasted. But they didn't. Instead they asked the dangerous question, "Where can we position ourselves in the mission field God's given us to most effectively make disciples?"

The answer to that simple but profound question gets at the heart of what it means to be fully present and engaged where we are, to see with fresh eyes opportunities and people God has put in our path.

For the Colemans, their answer was not what you and I might expect. But on further reflection, their response was so intentional, strategic, and fruitful. It was a play taken directly out of Jesus' playbook to be present wherever we are. It spoke volumes to the priority they place on relational discipleship.

Picture the dormitory where most students live. Loud, smelly, and often juvenile. Quite the opposite of the life empty nesters wait years for. Yet if you could pick just one strategic place where students spend the majority of their time in community doing life together, the dorm is it.

Now picture Dr. Coleman and his wife taking up residence in that dormitory . . . not for just one semester but for seven years. Dr. Coleman told me, "Where else could we spend that much time with the students? We were able to do life with them. We were able to speak into their lives in a way far more significant than what a few hours in a classroom can do. We chose the dorm room right next to the laundry room. The machines cost twenty-five cents and the students never had change. My wife kept a jar of coins for students so when they came around we could more easily engage in conversation."

Wait for the students to come to you for an hour or two a week in class, or go to them where they live?

Eternity looks different because the Colemans took seriously their general calling to be disciples who make disciples where they are. They rolled up their sleeves and thought like missionaries in the context God gave them. We need to do the same.

Daydreaming and praying for an elusive future in a place different than where we are can be the biggest threat to engaging the life and opportunities God puts directly in front of us. Rather than looking beyond what we have and are called to be stewards of, we should take ownership of what we've been given.

How we see life where we already are makes all the difference. If the classroom is our mission field, then teaching for a few hours per week is our focus. But if making disciples of students is the mission field, then the priority for living relationally in that context changes. If we are to be the best possible stewards of our general calling, we must be intentional where we are and see with new eyes.

Like Esther, God may have put us in a context where we already have the connections and position necessary for amazing generational impact (see Esther 4:14). We have to look with new eyes and find the courage to do what we can today to make a difference.

Already Positioned

Be a disciple who makes disciples where we are!

It's no accident that we have a context or core position (cP). We were born in this generation, with our native language, to a nationality, a culture, a family, and a set of early experiences that God ordained for us as a starting point.

As such, the first big question of GO is this: Where should I be a disciple who makes disciples?

It may surprise you to know that you currently have over fifty relationships of influence (or potential influence) where you are. These are the people you know by name and that you do life with. These are workmates, families, friends, and social circles that we intersect with, often on a daily basis.

What would happen if we began to think differently and see these relationships as our mission field for calling?

We often dream big related to calling, and that's good. Yet Jesus is continually pulling us back to the current moment. He says, "Whoever can be trusted with very little can also be trusted with much" (Luke 16:10), and this element of calling is incredibly relevant. How are we to serve and be faithful where we are now?

Jesus had just sent the disciples out two by two to neighboring villages to practice what they were learning. They returned excited and shared all they had experienced with Jesus. The apostle Mark gives us the account of their return. What unfolds encourages me while simultaneously wearing me out.

Mark reports that Jesus invited his disciples to retreat to a desolate place to get away from people and enjoy some rest. But the crowds followed them. Jesus had compassion because the crowds were like sheep without a shepherd, and he began to teach them. The disciples responded exactly the way you or I would when Jesus engaged the crowd. "No, Jesus. Not now. Later. Send them away. We are tired. What about that retreat to a desolate place? We've been working so hard."

Think about how you feel when you've returned from a long trip. It's late and you just want to sleep. That is exactly how the disciples felt. So when Jesus told them to feed the people, it wasn't exactly the first (or even hundredth) activity they'd prefer to be doing. Yes, there was a wonderful opportunity where they were going but an even more important need right where they were.

We need to see the feeding of the five thousand as the miracle of multiplication. See it through the lens of the backstory involving a tired and worn-out group of disciples ministering to the needs of people. The mission field where they engaged people was the context and opportunity for Jesus to work a miracle. In the same way, our mission field of everyday life creates a context for Jesus to show his grace, mercy, and power. We are the conduits of his love and his fullness where we are.

So what is our core position (cP)? Where we are!

Our primary or general calling that is common to all Christians, everywhere, all the time, is to make disciples in whatever context we find ourselves. We are to be good stewards of what God has already placed in our lives where we currently are.

Rethinking GO

Jesus said, "Go and make disciples of all nations" (Matthew 28:19). So how do we discern whether we should stay where we are or go somewhere new? Our natural inclination is to dream about a context beyond our current one.

Every GO that moves us physically and geographically simply puts us in a new local place to be a disciple who makes disciples where we are. We may be asked to pack our bags and GO. But when we are, it's for the purpose of creating a new local place or core position (cP) for carrying out our core mission (cM) to make disciples.

We must always remember that our calling finds its significance in the core mission for which it's given. Our unique gifting, good works and deeds, and place to engage are all important, but they are secondary to our central purpose: to be a disciple who makes disciples where we are.

Remember that Jesus spent nearly his entire three years of ministry within the equivalent of a major US metropolitan area. From Nazareth where he was born to Capernaum and its surrounding villages, where he did much of his public ministry, is about twenty miles. We can be certain that no matter where he traveled, he was making disciples. The apostle Peter settled in Jerusalem and made disciples while Paul traveled throughout neighboring countries planting the gospel. Some are to stay and some are to go, but either way we are to make disciples where we are.

What if "go" is really about engaging our calling? As we've discussed, the mission of the church is to carry the fullness of Jesus into every corner of society. That mission finds its context wherever we physically locate ourselves in the world. You might say our calling has an element of "plug and play." We plug in wherever we are and make disciples.

Recall our Ephesians 2:10 "sweet spot" that includes the "Be," "Do," and "Go" elements of calling. In the New King James Version it says, "We are his workmanship [BE], created in Christ Jesus for good works [DO], which God prepared beforehand that we should walk in them [GO]." To "walk in" is to engage.

Like Abraham, Jonah, and others, many of us will be called by God to physically GO somewhere new and risky. Consider two things as that journey unfolds. First, prepare (in practical ways) to say "yes" when that call to GO comes! Second, intentionally and strategically engage now, where you are, like Dr. Coleman did in that college dorm, in order to be the best possible steward of the field God has already placed you in. God will teach you things now that will amplify your effectiveness in the move to come. Are you waiting without engaging?

If so, it's time to get in the game!

All or Nothing

Making disciples is not an all-or-nothing journey. We don't need twelve men who drop their nets and follow us full-time. Obviously a willing and committed relationship like Jesus had with the disciples and Dr. Coleman had with his students is ideal for discipleship. But God knows where we are and who we are to impact. We need to work with what's been given to us. While the transformative work of Jesus in a person's life certainly requires surrender, the process of discipleship starts long before a person ever embraces Jesus.

Recall the elements of disciple making from the last chapter. They do not require that a person know or trust Jesus as a prerequisite. What is required is the fullness of Jesus in us intersecting with another person. The primary element is relational proximity. As long as the other person can see the influence of the fullness of Jesus in us, then they can be discipled.

Don't buy it? Ask ten people who know Jesus to tell you their story of coming to faith. Press into their stories to find the people and events that paved the way for their ultimate decision. Often you will find divine moments with people in their lives who overflowed with the fullness of Jesus, causing them to say something like, "I want what Dr. Coleman has!" When those far from God see the fruit of the fullness of Jesus in us, they will naturally want it.

Don't underestimate the influence the fullness of Jesus in us has on others when they see it.

Consider the son or daughter whom you love and have raised for sixteen years who is now rebelling and running from Jesus. They are not shy in letting you know that they don't believe in your Jesus or your faith. Are you discipling them amidst their rebellion or are you waiting for them to find Jesus? Of course you are discipling them. You pray and look for every opportunity to influence your child, even when you cannot control their actions. When we see with the eyes of Jesus, we have no option but to disciple.

We are missionaries to our children and spouses regardless of where they are spiritually. We can't control their receptivity to our words or even their desire to spend time with us, but we do disciple them by how they see the fullness of Jesus in us. The same should be true of others in our mission field.

If God is drawing your heart to a specific person, then be intentional with that person. Let the fullness of Jesus in you be a testimony to them. Be patient. Listen and pray for them like a missionary. Don't try to take more control than they've invited you to take, but make the most of every opportunity to let the light of Jesus shine through you.

Disciple making is not an all-or-nothing journey in which we need to wait on the other person to show receptivity. Start where you are with what you have. Embrace your mission field and a lifestyle of disciple making, seeking every opportunity for your life to carry the fullness of Jesus to others.

Seeing with Intentional and Strategic Eyes

A few years ago, author and missiologist Alan Hirsch challenged me with some seemingly simple questions. The conversation went something like this.

Alan: Who are you pastoring that is far from God?

Me: ?

Alan: Where are you spending the most time each week with people far from God?

Me: The gym. I go five to six times per week. I tend to go at the same times and see the same people.

Alan: What would it look like for you to become the pastor of the gym? What if you simply ordained or declared yourself the Gym Chaplain or Missionary to Gym? No permissions required. Just declare yourself as the owner of the role. Create a business card for yourself. In assuming that role, how would you become as effective as possible?

These pointed questions challenged my thinking. Until that moment, the gym had been an activity on my to-do list to get checked off each day. As an introvert, I counted success as getting in and out as quickly as possible, with no conversations to slow me down. That required going when the fewest number of people were there. As a patron of the gym, I never needed to get to know the staff or other members. But as a missionary to the gym, I had new responsibilities and concerns. As I began to think through the principles taught to missionaries and church planters, a new way of seeing and engaging my time at the gym emerged.

I interviewed a veteran judge who is living in the fullness of his calling. He sees his courthouse as his church. Not a church in the conventional sense for preaching and running Bible classes, but as a place for his staff and his community to see the fullness of Jesus in him. He sees his salutatory role as judge, but his functional role as a missionary and disciple maker. Seeing himself as the pastor of the courthouse is a game changer.

Do you believe there is an equivalent place or mission field for you? Possibly a context you have now that you simply need to embrace in a completely different way?

We must embrace the truth that there is a unique mission field where we are. When we do, we see our day-to-day lives very differently. From there, the opportunities to be intentional and strategic, partnering with what God is doing, become much easier to discern.

My Mission Field

So if my first priority is the mission field where I am now, how do I get started? I suggest two simultaneous pathways of discovery and engagement.

First, God has entrusted specific people and relationships to our care. We have a spiritual responsibility to family members and friends. These people are at the heart of our core position (cP). Make a list of 3–5 key people in your life with whom you *should* have a close relationship (even if it is currently strained). Do you see discipleship as your primary role in these relationships? Do your actions and approach support that? Are you being the fullness of Jesus to your spouse and kids? Are you really listening and engaging and modeling in a way that helps them see the love of God in you?

Second, discover where you need to be intentional and strategic beyond family and close friends. Our core position (cP) or mission field extends beyond our immediate family. Look for your "freshman dormitory" or "gym" context. Ask yourself questions like Alan Hirsch asked me. If you carried a business card that said, "Missionary to [fill in blank]" or "Disciple maker of [fill in blank]," what context might be the most fruitful? There is no one right answer. As you prayerfully consider the answer, God may reveal numerous possibilities to you. In fact, the opportunities are greater than your available time. The important thing is that you begin to think differently and that you engage in discipleship as a lifestyle, not as an activity.

Spend time praying through and defining your mission field. A good missionary spends as much time as needed to learn the culture and the context in which they serve. Spend time now intentionally and strategically defining the mission field that already exists in the rhythms of your life.

Getting Intentional

We had never heard of Chris Wienand as we sat among a group of pastors talking about planting more churches. Chris introduced himself and said, "My church is seven years old and may never grow above five hundred in attendance. But we've started over seventy churches." I don't think any of us believed it at first. You know how pastors sometimes exaggerate their math.

As we interrogated Chris, we found a story strikingly similar to Dr. Coleman's. "We don't have to create new strategies; we just need to do what Jesus did. One disciple at a time," Chris told us. Then he went on to say, "My church gives me the context to come invest in twelve different leaders each year. Discipleship is the goal and sending them to plant churches an outcome. By God's grace we've been able to do that for seven years in a row, thereby planting over seventy churches."

See the pattern? Jesus gave us a simple method. It works. Come alongside a small group and make disciples. Be a disciple who makes disciples where you are.

Be bold and intentional. Don't wait for special training or newfound fads. Look at the position you're already in with new eyes, and embrace God's heart to GO!

Mapping My Relational Influence: Applying the Calling Lens

As we've discussed, most of us already have over fifty relationships of influence in our lives. Applying this lens of calling involves a few simple steps.

First, make a list of all the titles and roles you currently play in life. For me these include things like husband, father, son, uncle, nephew, boss, coworker, coach, gym member, team member, and so on. Stretch your thinking and expand the list to roles where you have the capacity to influence relationally. For example, you might be a regular at Starbucks. The barista actually knows your name and what you normally drink. You've even found yourself engaged in conversations about life. Add "Starbucks Customer" to your list. If any role or title gives you enough relational equity to say, "Can I sit down with you for a few minutes to get your opinion on something?" then add it to your list.

Second, for each role and title on your list, add the names of specific people you have the opportunity to relationally influence. If you don't know all their names, simply put them generically on the list. For example, you might be the coach of your son's soccer team. You could add the names of each child plus their parents to your list. Most people will end up with over fifty names to consider.

Third, reflect on new roles or titles you don't currently have but could take on that would strategically give you access to relational influence. Maybe you've considered starting a new hobby club at work or college preparation group at church. What new roles could you assume that would connect you with others in a context built around something you are passionate about or love doing? Add these to your list.

Fourth, begin to apply the lens of calling. Use the following diagram to "map" your list. Each small circle is a role or title and each line is a person or relationship. Let

Where I am

GO

Discovering my general mission field!

the map simmer as you pray over it and continue adding to it. The map represents your current mission field. Use it to discover and consider specific opportunities to engage.

Fifth, rethink personal calling in the context of primary or general calling. Recall that our secondary or unique personal calling is God's gift to help us be more effective at engaging our general calling to make disciples where we are. It's our unique personal calling—we are uniquely made for specific good works and deeds where we can be most effective—that helps define how we can most effectively engage our mission field. In the remaining chapters, we'll look at each of the three elements of our unique personal calling.

In previous chapters we saw that our primary or general calling—shared by all Christians, everywhere, all the time—is to be disciples (BE), who make disciples (DO), wherever we are (GO). This general calling gives us a target for bringing our unique personal calling to life.

In the next few chapters we turn our attention from the general calling we share with all Christians to our unique personal calling: we are uniquely made (BE), to do good works and deeds (DO), wherever we can be most effective (GO).

In the following chapter we take a deeper look at the first element of our secondary or unique personal calling, our unique identity (uI).

Visit www.personalcalling.org for supplemental resources.

CHAPTER 12

Crafted by God: My Unique Identity

(Child of God)

Before I formed you in the womb I knew you,
before you were born I set you apart;
I appointed you as a prophet to the nations.

JEREMIAH 1:5

Secondary Calling = ul + uM + uP (BE   DO   GO)

Secondary Calling. Who am I created to BE? What is my unique identity (ul)?

My family loves watching reruns of the television show *MacGyver*. One attraction is Secret Agent MacGyver's uncanny ability to work his way out of hopeless life-and-death situations. How? By using common, everyday items that most of us take for granted. MacGyver uses the ordinary to create the extraordinary.

We find encouragement in MacGyver's ingenuity and persistence because down deep we all long for our lives to be more than common. But most of us are more like the cast of

Gilligan's Island, captive to our circumstances, doubting that we could ever truly experience the extraordinary. Possibly one of the most damaging lies Satan whispers in our ears is, "You are not unique and special!" This lie robs us of the abundance we were made to experience.

A pivotal and rich discovery in my journey to understanding calling comes from Jesus' own words in John 10:10. This verse actually inspired the title of this book. Jesus said, "The thief cometh not, but for to steal, and to kill, and to destroy: I am come that they might have life, and that they might have it more abundantly" (KJV). Some translations use the words "to the full" or "to the fullest measure" rather than "abundantly."

We are intrigued by the promise of experiencing life to its fullest measure, yet it's an elusive pursuit for most people. The chasm between having life and taking hold of it to the fullest measure is what caused you to read this book. While we are naturally drawn to the promise of living more abundantly, we can easily miss the subtle meaning of the qualifier that precedes it.

In the original Greek, the root word for "to have" can take several possessive forms. We can passively "have" life and easily take it for granted. To take hold of life more abundantly requires an active posture on our part. The pathway from merely having life to experiencing it to the fullest measure requires that we take hold of and steward our unique personal calling.

Also, notice in John 10:10 that the thief's role is active. He comes to steal, kill, and destroy. He uses our passivity and uncertainty against us. Our response must move us from "having" to "taking hold." We must not allow Satan's lies to confuse and paralyze us. We must actively take hold of our uniqueness not only as a truth from Scripture but also as a gift from God to be stewarded.

Consider Stephen, who has twenty years' experience climbing the corporate ladder and pursuing the good life. He enjoys the luxuries of life, including his "toys" (cars, boats, and jet skis). He is good at what he does and successful by the world's standards. His track record of promotions helps fuel his lifestyle but also holds him hostage. He experiences an emptiness and lack of satisfaction that lingers even as he conquers the next deal.

We choose in this life what we take hold of. It takes intentionality and discipline to take hold of the right things. Otherwise, the world's ways will take hold of us. God is the giver of good things in life, but he wants us to actively take hold of the better things he's made available to us. It starts with taking hold of our uniqueness, as a gift of God to be used for his purposes. When we embrace our uniqueness, we discover the path to living in our sweet spot of design.

Embracing Our Uniqueness

To be unique is to be special, to be one of a kind. This is even true physically. Scientists tell us it's mathematically impossible to have an exact copy of our DNA. The Bible says our uniqueness is not by chance. Instead God knew and saw us before we were substance in the womb; he envisioned our lives before we came into this world (Psalm 139:13–16; Galatians 1:15–16). We are his unique workmanship, intentionally and lovingly created as a work of his own hands. The image of a potter's hands crafting the clay into something beautiful is the story of our beginning (Job 10:8–9; Isaiah 64:8; Ephesians 2:10).

These truths of a unique core identity (cI) are promises for today and not shallow, poetic words of mere inspiration.

In our heads we know the truth, but in our hearts we struggle to fully embrace it. Our uniqueness is a special gift from the one who envisioned us before we were ever conceived in the womb. Somewhere between the head and the heart, we become confused about who we were created to be, resulting in our hands never engaging what we were created to do.

Good sets us apart!

God sets us apart and calls us to accomplish good works that he prepared for us to do before we breathed our first breath, and he wants us to do those works in relationship with him. We are sacred and set apart, because the One who is sacred made us and has a unique mission (uM) or purpose for our lives (Jeremiah 1:5; Galatians 1:15–16; Ephesians 1:4; 4:11).

We are uniquely made. Our birth was not an accident. God planned us for a specific purpose. *God has a plan + a purpose for us!*

Overflow

But why would God do it this way? He could have created an army of conformist robots to serve as his thoughtless pawns. Instead he chose to (1) equip us for an eternal, intimate love relationship with himself and (2) equip us to uniquely participate and play our part in his purposes and mission here on earth: to love other people.

There is an overflow from the first to the second.

When Jesus was asked about the greatest commandments, he said, "'Love the Lord your God with all your heart and with all your soul and with all your mind.' This is the first and greatest commandment. And the second is like it: 'Love your neighbor as yourself'" (Matthew 22:37–39). Our love relationship with Jesus leads us to put love into action by loving other people. The overflow of Jesus' love for us (and ours for him) should result in love for other people.

The principle of overflow is also embedded in John 10:10. The Greek for "more abundantly" means filled beyond measure or filled to overflowing. This sense of "more" is exceedingly, abundantly more. The Greek means "more than enough; filled to overflowing." Love can and should overflow from us to others. Paradoxically it's the overflow to others that lets us experience the personal abundance Jesus promises.

Jesus doesn't just tell us we should love God and love people; he equips us to take hold of it. Recall from Ephesians 1:22–23 that a core purpose for the church is to carry the fullness of Jesus into every crack and cranny of society. It's our uniqueness that gives each of us a specific role that only we can accomplish in God's bigger plan for reaching the world. God's unique handiwork in our lives gives us each a unique identity (uI) that is to abundantly overflow to others as we GO.

Our primary or general calling gives us the fullness of Jesus and a context for what we are to accomplish when we go (i.e., a definition of success). This overflows to our secondary or unique calling, equipping us to play our unique part. This comes, not by force of will, but rather as a movement of love, one act of kindness at a time. It is carried out by uniquely made people taking hold of their unique part in bringing the fullness of Jesus to a lost and hurting world.

In their book *Live Your Calling*, Kevin and Kay Brennfleck write, "Our calling is to travel through life with God, living each day as called people. We are unique and set-apart people, overflowing with good works prepared for us to do as we live each day."[1] This is the harmony flowing from calling to good works.

Our unique identity (uI) of BE is the first element in our secondary or unique personal calling. We must discover it, embrace it, and allow it to guide how we steward the time, talent, treasure, and influence God gives us in doing good works and deeds. It is from the overflow of our unique design that God brings our unique good works to life.

Our Unique Identity (uI)

While we can never completely define the fullness of our uniqueness, we can seek to express it in a short phrase. Our unique identity (uI) is a word or phrase that seeks to capture the fullness of our unique design in very simple terms. You might be a creative storyteller, or an encouraging coach, or a restorer of broken relationships, or a collaborative networker. The possibilities and descriptors are endless and reflect the breadth of God's creativity brought to life in our uniqueness.

I'm an "entrepreneurial engineer." My unique identity related to calling is captured in these two words. This expression has evolved through the years, and I will likely continue to tweak it. But the essence of my design is somewhere close to the characteristics of an entrepreneur and an engineer. This is a lens through which I can see the world and seek to better understand my past, present, and future.

How do we discover our unique identity (uI)? We look for clues. In coaching people to discover their unique design, several practical tips have proven helpful. These include:

1. Our lives are like a book. The clues of our unique identity (uI) are spread throughout the story being written in our lives, from birth until now.
2. The clues transcend all domains of life including personal, family, work, church, and community. The characteristics are illuminated 24/7. We can't turn them off.
3. There are assessment tools we can use to help uncover and then to magnify the clues.

The following subsections provide more detail on these truths.

TIP 1: SEE YOUR LIFE AS A BOOK TO READ

If we desire clarity on who we are and where our story is headed, we should first look to the past for clues revealed in what's already been lived. The first twenty-five chapters of our story give us the best perspective on where chapters 26 and 27 are headed. The clues scattered throughout our past shed light on God's unique workmanship and his divine plans for our future. We must learn to look for them, integrate them, and learn from them just as an investigator looks for clues.

My passion for pursuing my calling was ignited by the Paterson Life Planning Process, created by the world-renowned business strategist Tom Paterson. Master Life Plan facilitator Pete Richardson was helping me unpack the story

God had written in my life and where that story was headed in the next chapter. As Pete highlighted over fifteen different entrepreneurial initiatives I'd started, he said, "You are a serial kingdom entrepreneur and engineer."

Yes. An entrepreneurial engineer. It's that simple. My core identity is not something I can turn on and off. It's always with me. Whether I'm sitting in meetings, coaching a sports team, surfing the Internet, or cutting my grass, I'm dreaming up new ventures and plotting strategy for existing ones.

As you look at the chapters God has already written in your life, pay particular attention to those moments you recall with vividness. These are often turning points in our lives that can give solid insights into who we are at our core. These turning points are like the fingerprints left at a crime scene ready for discovery.

"I remember when" moments are beacons crying out that give us deeper insights into who we are uniquely made to be. We have thousands of experiences that integrate into our story, but only a handful that vividly and clearly shout, "I remember when . . ." Pay particular attention to them.

What seems so obvious now had been lying idle in the clues of my story, waiting to be discovered and brought to life in fuller measure. The clarity we seek is not hard to discover if we are willing look more deliberately at the part of our stories that has already been lived. Clarity is found in the patterns of the past. In retrospect, the clues pointing to "entrepreneurial engineer" are embedded throughout my story.

Before I was five years old, I remember taking the living room coffee tables apart and putting them back together. I was inquisitive and loved to see how things worked and fit.

As early as I can remember, I wanted to be an architect. At the time, I couldn't tell you why since I was not an artist and didn't like to draw. However, there was something about taking a blank sheet of paper and bringing a vision of the future to life that tugged on my heart.

I remember the day and the moment in seventh grade when my dreams of being an architect gave way to a new dream. My science teacher stood next to a blank board and drew an atom (neutrons, protons, and electrons). He described the atom in detail and explained how we can harness the energy of atoms when they split. How could someone know so much about something they'd never seen and then draw a picture of it? I was mesmerized. I went home that day believing I wanted to be a nuclear physicist.

Looking back, my interest had nothing to do with a nuclear physicist's work. It had everything to do with a teacher drawing a picture of something futuristic and powerful that he had never himself seen. Sounds unmistakably similar to the core characteristics of an architect who draws images of future possibilities. Two distinct memories, each pointing to a common core aspect of my design.

When I was about thirteen, my father planted hedges around the back of our yard. I was assigned "irrigation duty" to water those hedges after school each day. It took a long time to manually water the long line of new hedges. As I worked and watched my friends play, a thought popped into my head. "Why don't you dig a trough connecting the base of the hedges in one channel and run a hose from the back of the house to the high point of the channel?" I was able to position the hose, turn the water on, go play, and let gravity complete my chores.

Instead of frowning on my apparent laziness, my parents encouraged my ingenuity. They said, "You are a natural engineer and problem solver." My ambition to become a nuclear physicist gave way to a desire to become a nuclear engineer—an ambition that I achieved after college when I was hired at the Division of Naval Reactors.

Years later when God was calling me into full-time ministry, I dragged my feet for two full years. Why? Ministry appeared inconsistent with my core essence as an "entrepreneurial engineer." Ministry felt like a dead end for a strategic futurist engineer. I remember vividly the day

God said, "Trust me," even though the decision to leave my engineering career made no worldly sense. Sometimes God works that way. Little did I see that this step of faith would actually release the latent entrepreneur in me and mature me to the next level of understanding and engagement of my unique personal calling.

Inquisitive tinkerer to would-be architect to would-be nuclear physicist to nuclear engineer to kingdom entrepreneur. At first glance this path may seem disjointed, but it is not. When you press into each role and look at what caused excitement in my soul, a common theme emerges. All of these roles involve understanding today's reality, seeing a preferable future, and engineering or shaping a pathway to get there.

I don't have to take fifty different tests to figure that out. The clues are already embedded in the story of my life and reveal themselves in all domains of life. I just have to slow down, find the clues, and pursue the deeper understanding of how they fit together. The same is true for you.

TIP 2: FIND THE CLUES THAT TRANSCEND ALL DOMAINS OF LIFE

The fingerprints of our unique identity (uI) and design transcend all the domains of our life, including our relationship with God, self, family, work, church, and community. The unique elements of our core gifting are embedded in our DNA. We can't turn them on and off. While they may show themselves more prominently in one domain of life, their imprints are everywhere. They travel with us and influence our thoughts, decisions, and actions.

My oldest son Ben is one of the smartest people I know. From the time he could read, he was devouring "How Things Work" books. When he was five years old, we lived in a house with a septic sewer system. Ben took my mother into the bathroom, pressed the "flusher" on the toilet, and proceeded to explain how the entire system worked. "It goes down the toilet and through pipes in the basement. It then goes out to a tank in the front yard. Water in that tank overflows through another pipe to the septic field out on the side yard. From there it is distributed to our yard."

Huh? I don't think any of the rest of us really understood it. Intellect, inquisitiveness, and deliberative thinking are embedded in Ben's core DNA. He is gifted with tons of smarts and an inquisitive nature. He is a "deliberative, contemplative thinker" who lives inside his thought life. This unique identity transcends his personal life, his family life, his work life, his church role, and his engagement in the broader community. It shapes who he is uniquely made to be. The same is true of you and me. God made us with core elements of identity that touch every aspect of life.

When we read the story of our lives as a book, from birth until today, looking for the core characteristics of our design that are always there jumping into action across all domains of life, we create a lens for discovering our unique identity (uI). Grab hold of what you know to be true without worrying about having the perfect words today. As a young college student just entering the workforce, my son Ben's understanding and refinement of his unique identity will mature and be refined with time and experience. "Deliberative, contemplative thinker" is simply a starting point.

TIP 3: USE PERSONAL ASSESSMENT TOOLS . . . CAREFULLY

Although our life story holds most of the clues we need to dis-cover our unique gifting, there are numerous self-assessment tools that can enhance our discovery and understanding of our personal wiring. No single assessment is the "silver bul-let" or "magic formula." Instead, think of each as one of many possible avenues of discovery.

There are many free and fee-based assessment tools available online. Take advantage of the free ones, but know that most of the fee-based ones provide detailed reports that are worth the cost. Visit www.personalcalling.org to see a list of suggested tools and to download supplemental resources.

Most tools such as DISC, Myers Briggs, and Strengths-Finder have distinct categories or "types" that you are matched to. These profiles are based on taking the complexity of a large population of data and reducing things to a manageable number of characteristics. Unfortunately, not all the characteristics within a profile or type will describe you perfectly. Be careful to only extract the elements that do.

Consider the wedding planner profiled as an introvert. She scores 51 percent introvert and 49 percent extrovert. Although her report will label her an introvert based on these results, that would be an incomplete characterization. Some of the descriptive characteristics will match her perfectly while others don't. This is the inherent weakness of assessment reports that cause some people to be cynical and result in their missing the clues that need to be discovered. The key is to extract the parts that do match and ignore the rest.

I encourage people to go through the assessment reports and highlight words that are a strong fit. Don't highlight descriptions that partially describe you, but only the ones that really nail you, the things your spouse and close friends would strongly agree with. After highlighting these descriptors, extract them into your own custom list or report. For each report you will likely get at least twenty-five words (or sentences) that strongly describe you.

In this way, the wedding planner described above would come up with some key words descriptive of an introvert and some of an extrovert. This is a more true representation of her unique design. Assessments tend to put us in black-and-white categories when our unique design is a color mosaic. The good news . . . if you are disciplined to extract the applicable words from three or more assessments, you will see a clear picture of the characteristics of your unique identity (uI) and design emerge.

In my personal experience of helping others discover their personal calling, two assessments have been particularly helpful in finding a person's unique design and gifting.

Natural Abilities (StrengthsFinder)

The Gallup organization has a wonderful tool called Strengths-Finder. The thirty-four different traits in their profile are based on research and feedback from millions of people all over the world. The assessment is available online for a small fee with options for getting a report of your top five traits or your full thirty-four in order (from most prevalent to least).

The concept of StrengthsFinder is simple. We are born with natural abilities or talents that are embedded in our DNA. We've been referring to these as our unique identity (uI) and design. When we further enhance our natural talents by adding knowledge and skill (developed proficiency) to the mix, we develop strengths.

I have found the reports to be remarkably accurate and insightful when you go through and extract the top five themes that strongly describe you. Especially helpful is the intuitive and memorable descriptive words they use. After taking StrengthsFinder, you will likely say, "Those words do describe me." These key words can then be integrated into a core word or phrase.

Consider Bill, a successful middle-aged leader wrestling with what's next for him. He'd worked his way up through his company to become CEO. He mastered numerous competencies along the way but found himself spending considerable time in activities that did not bring him natural joy. This is a significant clue that his current role may be misaligned from his unique core essence. This can happen over time as the organization promotes you or repositions you to their needs rather than your strengths. Bill is energized by playing a role in connecting people and opportunities for impact. His top StrengthsFinder characteristics are: Futuristic, Individualization, and Connectedness. See the future. See how individuals play unique roles. See how things connect together. Bill is a "bridge builder" for connecting people and future opportunities for impact.

Like Bill, most people can create an initial two-to five-word unique identity (uI) description simply by taking the StrengthsFinder tool and examining its results.

APEST (Fivefold Ministry) Assessment

Jesus not only calls us to carry his fullness into the world, he equips us with unique gifts to accomplish the mission. We find our identity in him, and part of that core identity (cI) is the unique gifts he gives each of us.

Paul writes, "Christ himself gave the apostles, the prophets, the evangelists, the pastors and teachers, to equip his people for works of service, so that the body of Christ may be built up until we all reach unity in the faith and in the knowledge of the Son of God and become mature, attaining to the whole measure of the fullness of Christ. . . . We will grow to become in every respect the mature body of him who is the head, that is, Christ. From him the whole body, joined and held together by every supporting ligament, grows and builds itself up in love, as each part does its work" (Ephesians 4:11–13; 15b–16).

These verses tell us that Jesus himself gives out five different gifts for the purpose of each person and the church reaching maturity in him. Each person receives a gift and has a unique part to play in the growth and maturity of the body. This gifting from Ephesians 4 is often referred to as the "fivefold ministry" or "APEST" (for Apostles, Prophets, Evangelists, Shepherds, and Teachers).

Which of the five gifts is most descriptive of you? Like other "profile" assessments, there will be elements of each of the five that describe you so be sure to extract the key elements from your report. There are a number of online tools for assessing which gifts you have. My friend and author Alan Hirsch is a strong advocate of APEST and has a tool on his Forgotten Ways website (theforgottenways.org).

Don't get stuck on the five specific words. Most people who are apostolically or prophetically gifted are reluctant to use these words about themselves. Don't let that create a barrier. Look beyond the specific labels to their meanings. Use a similar but different word than the label if that is more comfortable for you.

Alan Hirsch notes that apostles extend, prophets know, evangelists recruit, shepherds nurture and protect, and teachers understand and explain. Consider some prominent people you may know.

- Paul, an *apostle* who started churches far beyond Israel
- Martin Luther King, Jr., a *prophet* who proclaimed God's truth for a preferable future of fairness
- Billy Graham, an *evangelist* who called people to Jesus in huge stadium revivals all around the world
- Mother Theresa, a *shepherd* who cared for the "least of these" in third world poverty
- C. S. Lewis, a *teacher* of Christ Jesus, defending the gospel and reaching out to the reluctant and unconvinced

Here are lists of additional words that go with each of the five gifts:

APOSTOLIC
- Expand or Extend
- Establish
- Drive
- Scale and sustainability
- Design
- Provoke
- Systematize
- Strategic
- Pioneering
- Entrepreneur
- Explore
- Start
- Overcome
- Innovate
- Catalyze

PROPHETIC
- Illuminate
- Reveal
- Shape
- Proclaim
- Point
- Assess
- Pioneering
- Diagnose
- Align
- Challenge and correct
- Discern
- Justice
- Seeing possibilities/ visionary
- Perceptive
- Tell/Foretell

154

EVANGELISTIC

- Recruit and seek out
- Enthusiastic/Raving Fan
- "Living Invitation"
- Provoking Interest
- Advertising and PR
- Inspire
- Share/Tell
- Catalyze
- Persuade
- Salesman
- Proclaim
- Expand
- Connect
- Pioneering
- Entrepreneur

SHEPHERD

- Nurture and protect
- Operational
- Develop
- Empathize
- Technician, Operator, Counselor, Builder, etc.
- Caretaker
- Manage
- Calm
- Supporting
- Loyal
- Feed
- Comfort
- Help
- See and Serve

TEACHER

- Explain and enlighten
- Grasp and apply truth
- Transfer knowledge
- Show/Demonstrate
- Bridging theory and practice
- Understand
- Define
- Model
- Instill
- Exemplify
- Guide others
- Illustrate
- Develop
- Extract

Why did Jesus give these five gifts? We can't be sure, but they do cover the range of functions needed by most organizations. Jesus was strategic and knew the key gifts that would be needed to grow the church and accomplish his mission. Trust his provision and that you have received a unique gifting to equip you for his mission.

Don't see these as five all-or-nothing gifts into which you must nicely fit yourself into just one. Instead look beyond the five titles to the underlying traits to see the color mosaic that can be created by combining different characteristics from the different gifts. Few of us fit perfectly in one gift.

Consider John, a midcareer teacher who has won numerous "Teacher of the Year" awards. His students tend to do better on placement tests and have a higher graduation rate. He clearly has the gift of "Teacher." But if we look closer, we will find that he also has numerous strengths from each of the other four primary gifts. His unique makeup is a mosaic of traits from the primary gifts. The same is true for you and me.

The APEST assessment attempts to identify our top two primary gifts (e.g., Shepherd and Teacher). As noted previously, we are best served by reviewing the entire assessment results, including descriptions for all five primary gifts, and extracting the words that best describe us into our own custom report or list. This approach will help us create a description of our own unique gifts.

Application: The Lens of Unique Identity (uI)

Earlier, we introduced the idea of "lenses" for looking closely at each of the six dimensions of calling covered in this book. This lens is designed to help us identify characteristics of how we are uniquely created, the characteristics that uniquely define us and distinguish us from others.

From this list of descriptive words, we can craft a short description of our unique identity (uI) that is evident across all domains of life. Embrace this as a work in progress that you will refine over time. The initial one to five words may not be the words you use a year from now. Your clarity is a work in progress. My words have changed several times over the past few years, but their meaning have remained approximately the same.

Consider Emily, a twenty-four-year-old full of energy and ideals with a lifetime ahead of her. She graduated from college with good grades but was uncertain what to do next. She enjoyed pursuing her history degree, but it didn't open up any job offers to help her pay the student loans. She's now an hourly wage earner to pay the bills while she figures out what she really wants to do. She is genuinely burdened that she is not being a good steward of her natural gifting or her formal training.

As you read through the suggested exercise below, notice how Emily's core identity (uI) reveals itself. Consider how the "clues" point to her core identity. Take the time to work through the exercise for yourself. You can visit www. personalcalling.org to see additional examples of this exercise in action.

Step 1: Look more deeply into the story God has already written in your life. There are a number of exercises at www. personalcalling.org to assist you in looking for and discerning clues from your story. Use these completed worksheets as you work through the remaining steps below. Let me encourage you not to skip this step. Take the time to map out at least the high-level highlights of the story God has already written in your life. Consider brainstorming the following list from events in your life. Give each item on your list a date (or date range) and title.

- Significant life events (e.g. births, deaths, marriage, spiritual conversion, and so on)
- Jobs and work experience
- Moves (especially the ones that changed the context of your local mission field)
- School/education
- Awards, achievements, certifications, promotions, and notable affirmations (anything acknowledging a distinctive accomplishment)
- "I remember when . . ." moments (the vivid ones that you remember even years later)
- Health issues and illnesses
- Seasons of spiritual highs and lows
- Volunteer and community service activities
- Hobbies and extracurricular activities

Take the time to work through these lists, spending as little as five minutes on each one. Consider consolidating the lists into a single, comprehensive timeline of your life. Visual people may want to put the timeline on large sheets taped to the wall to see the full picture. You will be surprised at the progress you can make *and* this exercise will prove fruitful in helping you extract key clues in the remaining steps below.

Our store clerk Emily, burdened that her natural gifts were underutilized, discovered the following when she worked through the "I remember when . . ." exercise:

- Visiting the American History Museum. I could have stayed there for weeks soaking up the history.
- Going on field trips during elementary school to historic places. I could see the information in my textbooks come to life
- "Consuming" history documentaries on television. I remember wishing I could watch these shows rather than attend school.
- Enjoying classes where I really seemed to gain insights into the context for how things are today. I would connect past history to today's reality.

Notice how the common thread of "history and context" is woven throughout Emily's most vivid memories.

Step 2: Take several personal assessments including StrengthsFinder and APEST. As your time and budget permit, complete additional self-discovery tools such as DISC or Myers Briggs. Each tool creates additional vantage points for looking more closely at your unique design. The great thing is that you can continue taking and adding more tools to your discovery library throughout your life. Visit www. personalcalling.org for additional resources and to use a free tool for aggregating your assessment results into a personal dashboard library.

Emily's StrengthsFinder assessment revealed the following:

- Learner
- Connectedness (seeing links between things)
- Context (understand present by looking at the past)
- Responsibility
- Adaptability (flexible)

"Learner" is one word that Emily believes captures her core. The "connectedness" and "context" traits amplify and enhance her love of learning.

Meanwhile, Emily's APEST assessment revealed these two characteristics:

- Shepherd
- Teacher

It's important to contextualize the APEST gifts to your life. For example, "shepherds" can take on many forms of caring for people, processes, and things. Emily senses she is a shepherd in a similar way that a librarian stewards the information in a library, organizing information so it can be accessed and distributed to make people and the world a better place. Emily uses the metaphor of being a high school librarian who is also a history teacher. Notice how her StrengthsFinder profile amplifies this.

Step 3: Review the full reports and extract or create a more focused, custom list of key words and phrases that strongly describe you. Don't highlight anything that is only moderately true and/or not prevalent most of the time across all the domains of your life. Extract the keywords and phrases into a comprehensive list that becomes your working report.

Emily might extract words and phrases like the following:

- drawn to the process of learning
- the outcome of learning is less significant than the journey of getting there
- connectedness is everywhere and ours to discover
- understanding and extracting knowledge energizes me
- views the world through a lens of knowledge and understanding
- loves teaching and creating environments of learning
- loves the challenge of integrating and connecting just the right information
- enjoys working with details

Step 4: Seek to group similar or like words into a single word that best describes that grouping. For example, *bold*, *fearless*, *daring*, and *risk-taking* may reduce to one of those words or even a new word like *adventuresome*.

Emily condenses her words to the following key words: *learning*, *discovery*, *knowledge*, *integrating*, and *connecting*.

Step 5: Take a stab at condensing your insights from steps 1–4 into a two-to five-word phrase that describes your unique identity (uI) and design. You may end up using a word directly from one of the assessments. Use words and phrases that are memorable or personally significant for you. Select words that seem to apply across all domains of life (e.g., personal, work, family), and don't be paralyzed by thinking you need a perfect phrase.

Emily's Unique Identity: At her core, she's an INQUISITIVE LEARNER.

An "inquisitive learner" could do thousands of different things in thousands of different places. Armed with her unique identity (uI) of inquisitive learner, Emily can then focus on understanding her unique mission (uM) for putting that gifting in use and her unique position (uP) to discover where she can be the best steward of her secondary or unique calling.

To live within her unique sweet spot of calling, Emily will need to find a career path that activates her inquisitive learner profile!

In the example above, I've only included a sampling of the applicable key words for Emily. Your job is to begin building a comprehensive picture using key word and phrase descriptors then focus them to reveal your unique identity (uI). The process of gaining clarity will continue into the future. Be intentional and let the process begin today!

Pause

Reflect on your unique identity (uI) and design. Can you boil it down to five words or less? Don't worry if it feels obscure.

Your discovery of personal calling is a work in progress. Before moving forward, write down in five words or less a description of your unique BE. Give yourself permission to change it tomorrow so that you don't become paralyzed.

Calling is lived out as our unique identity (uI) translates into action.

What we do flows out of who we are. Specifically, our unique mission (uM), expressed in our good works and deeds, overflows from our unique identity (uI), as discussed in the last chapter. In the following chapter we take a deeper look at the question, "What is my unique mission (uM)?"

Visit www.personalcalling.org for supplemental resources.

CHAPTER 13

Good Works and Deeds: My Unique Mission

[May God] make you worthy of his calling,
and . . . by his power [may he] bring to fruition your
every desire for goodness and your every deed
prompted by faith.

2 THESSALONIANS 1:11

Secondary Calling. What am I created to DO?
What is my unique mission (uM)?

At seventeen, I worked as a part-time groundskeeper at my high school. It was a Saturday morning like most others, and my supervisor and I were walking the grounds. My supervisor was a quiet and reserved man who shared little about his life, but I knew he had served on the front lines of the Vietnam War. That day, in the space of five minutes, he burned a permanent memory in my mind while effortlessly saving the life of a young boy.

It all happened so fast but in what felt like slow motion. The young boy who rode past us on his bike was a daredevil, jumping curves and popping wheelies as he intersected our path. As proof that the male brain doesn't fully form until after the teen years, this young boy's bike had no seat. Instead, the one-inch diameter metal shaft that protruded directly upward from the bike frame to hold the seat formed a perfect spear projecting toward his body.

Got the picture? Bike. Metal spear sticking straight up from bike frame. Invincible daredevil youth.

The young thrill seeker rode up a set of steps, and back down again to jump off a several-foot high ramp at the bottom. He lost control and crashed. The metal pole sticking up from the frame pierced completely through his lower arm near the main arteries. A clean piercing entered on one side and exited the other. Blood was everywhere and gushing. The boy was screaming. He quickly went into shock.

While I was paralyzed and virtually useless, my calm and cool supervisor took control. He comforted and reassured the boy, applied pressure to the wound, and tied a tourniquet before I could even catch my breath. Fortunately, I was directed to go call the paramedics, guaranteeing my removal from the blood zone.

My supervisor was exactly the right person, in exactly the right place, at just the right time. Those years of hell on the front lines in Vietnam helped prepare him for his role in this very moment. If I were in that young boy's shoes, there is no one in the world I'd rather have had right there to help me in my moment of crisis. Part of my supervisor's purpose and destiny was to save that boy's life. This wasn't just something the man did; it was connected to his past, to who he was, and to what he was made to do.

In contrast, I knew in that moment that I was not called to work anywhere near blood!

God has given each of us gifts and abilities for the purpose of blessing others and joining his grand adventure in the world.

The needs are everywhere around us. Some are obvious and visible like the daredevil boy's medical emergency, but most lie seemingly dormant just below the surface. These needs are awaiting a divine encounter with just the right person at just the right time in just the right place. Some can be met with a kind word or helping hand, but most have their roots in people's need to find their way back to God.

In the landscape of possible activity, what if I'm just the right person to carry the fullness of Jesus to those in need in the mission field I already find myself in? What if my unique, ordained good works and deeds are God's invitation to a divine encounter with people far from himself? What if I need to stop seeing my unique mission (uM) as a single thing for a lifetime but rather a sacred stewardship of the opportunities in front of me today?

We are the right person, in the right place, at just the right time for someone today! My secondary or unique personal calling is less about the perfect match of some fairy-tale journey and more about my bias to act in faith and obedience to play my unique roles in carrying the fullness of Jesus to a lost and dying world. My unique mission is about faithfulness in expressing the fullness of Jesus as I look for the opportunity to serve others today.

Ordinary and Extraordinary

Think about times you have been the right person in the right place at the right time. Often these sacred moments are hidden in the mundane noise of our busy lives. There may have been hundreds of times throughout your life that you've unknowingly been the right person for someone else. There are also countless times that others have been that person for you. Too often, we just don't see such encounters with the weight of significance that they deserve.

Shortly before his death, Jesus needed a place to celebrate the Passover with his disciples. He said to two of his followers, "Go into the city, and a man carrying a jar of water will meet you. Follow him" (Mark 14:13). This nameless man led the disciples to the place where they'd spend some of their last, most precious hours with Jesus, hearing some of his richest teaching. We only know this man as the one carrying a jar. Yet his role was significant, even if he didn't know it!

At times you might be an innocent bystander playing an ordinary role that anyone willing to give of his or her time could do. At other times you might be just the right, extraordinary person for a given opportunity, as my supervisor was in saving that boy's life. In living out our unique personal calling, we simultaneously play ordinary and extraordinary roles. One is simply about being available and willing to give of ourselves, wherever we are needed. The other is about being a strategic, good steward of the unique gifting we've been given, exercising it with focus and intentionality. Both find context within the opportunities that cross our paths every day.

Are we willing to be nameless men and women carrying jars, faithful with both ordinary and extraordinary good works and deeds? If so, we will need to discern the unique good works and deeds designed for us and embedded in our personal calling as our unique mission (uM).

Rethinking Work

One of the most often asked questions when meeting someone is, "What do you do?" Our identity is disproportionately linked to what we do rather than who God created us to be. This finds its root in the fall of man and the three chasms created by sin. Recall that sin caused humanity to lose its: (1) identity in God (who we were created to be), (2) purpose in the world (what we were made to do), and (3) position in eternity.

In losing our divine purpose of serving God, our days became numbered and we were left to "toil" as we worked the earth to provide for ourselves. Toilsome work is a direct

166

consequence of sin. The good news is that Jesus bridges the chasm. We can once again experience meaningful and purposeful work. Our personal calling transcends all domains of our lives, making it possible for us to experience abundant life to the fullest measure. God equips us to once again find joy in the things that we do.

So why do we remain trapped in the toilsome paradigm, never discovering the divine good works and deeds God has for us? I believe there are two reasons. First, we never discover who God uniquely made us to BE (chapter 12). As a result, we drift along looking to discover a unique mission (uM) that we were made to DO without a proper context of it overflowing from who we were made to be.

Second, the system we grow up in creates a "rut" that is hard for us to break out of. We spend the first twenty years of life trying to figure out what we are good at. Our parents direct us toward specific activities, not always with the right motives. Unfortunately, we allow the DO and the realities of needing to make a living take priority over the BE of who we are. As a consequence, our unique mission (uM) never aligns and flows from our unique identity (uI). Instead of helping our children discover who they are at their core, we tend to direct them toward what they need to DO to be successful.

Most of our teens go off to college without understanding their unique identity, passions, burdens, and gifts. We spend lots of money to equip them for a life of "doing." But in an ill-fitting career path, they may become disillusioned and frustrated by a lack of joy and fulfillment. When they should be hitting their stride, many of them experience a midlife crisis, wondering if what they've been doing is really what they were meant to do. They live with a nagging discontent that keeps them from experiencing the abundant life Jesus says is available. The "rut" is deep and firmly established, so they begin dreaming of a more hopeful future in retirement. Work becomes a necessary evil to be tolerated rather than a sacred mission field to bless others and live out our calling.

There is a better way.

God intends and has made a way for us to experience full-measure, abundant living *now*, even in our vocation!

Think about this logically for a minute. Jesus calls us to live abundantly (John 10:10). He calls us to deploy what we have for eternal treasures, not to accumulate possessions here on earth (Matthew 6:19–20). He equips us with a unique design and good works (Ephesians 2:10) to have a meaningful role in his mission here on earth.

Trusting that these teachings of Jesus are true, why would he carve out an exception for our vocational work, the place we spend more time than anywhere else? Does he really intend for us to live abundantly, except in our work? To deploy for eternal treasure what's been entrusted to our care, except in our work? To fully use and engage our unique giftedness and good works, except in our work? Certainly not! He intends that we experience all these things in work. In fact, for many of us, work is our most ripe mission field for living out and expressing our personal calling.

Specialist or Generalist

Our unique mission (uM) may be a single cause or message that extends throughout our lifetime, or it may be a series of many good works and deeds that are loosely connected to a more general overarching theme. We see both in Scripture and in history.

Our unique identity (uI) and mission (uM) may draw us to a single, narrow focus. This was the case for Moses, David, Paul, Billy Graham, Mother Theresa, Martin Luther King, and William Wilberforce. God gave each of them a personal calling that was very focused for the long haul. They were specialists led by the siren call of a specific cause or theme.

But what about Jonah, who was called to Nineveh to preach repentance; or Nehemiah, who was called to Jerusalem to rebuild the walls; or Noah, who was called to build an ark; or Lydia, who was called to house Paul in

Philippi? They each had at least one special mission that only lasted a short period of their lives. What are we to assume about the rest of their lives? Is it likely that the same gifts they used in these special missions were also used in other ways? Nehemiah was a strong leader and strategic thinker. Was this gifting for a lifetime or for one short season?

Let this sink in. Calling is *not* necessarily about doing one thing the rest of your life. You may be blessed to have a common theme that helps unite your good works and deeds, but most of us need to see each day and each season as a stewardship of the opportunities in front of us in the mission field where we are. An overarching mission is often made up of many smaller missions deployed throughout the different seasons of our lives. Unfortunately, most people miss the continuous stream of opportunities that pass them by, while waiting for clarity on their calling. Good works and deeds require action . . . today . . . tomorrow . . . and every day.

While many of us will never have an epic mission that puts us in the spotlight of fame and glamor, we are extraordinary because we are uniquely made with unique missions assigned by our Creator. We may be generalists who are called to be faithful in numerous and varied missions rather than a single cause. If so, count that a blessing to add variety and spice to life. Seek to discover the overarching theme that shapes your unifying purpose.

Are you a specialist or a generalist? Not sure? That's okay. Let's press deeper into discovering our unique mission (uM) of good works and deeds.

Gut Check

Why do I do what I do vocationally (or why will I do it if I'm not currently in the workforce)? It's not by mistake we find ourselves where we are, doing what we do. Although the reasons and motives can be good and bad, there is a backstory that led you to where you are.

Pause and reflect on the following questions to candidly assess where you are now in the journey to living the purpose you were made for:

Question 1—Which of the following factors shape why you do what you currently do vocationally. If you are between jobs, identify the factors that will most significantly shape your pursuit. Rank these from the most to the least significant.

- Finances, benefits, and security
- Expectations and/or desires of others, including family members (e.g., parents wanting you to do what you do)
- Gifting and natural talents
- Passions and burdens
- Personal fulfillment and joy
- Legacy or impact
- Sense of purpose or significance
- Compatibility with vision, values, and beliefs
- Chance/fate
- Inheritance (e.g., continuing the family business)
- It's all that was available
- Sense of divine leading or intervention
- [insert your unique factors that are not on this list]

Which are most prominent? Do you have any motives that could keep you from living within your sweet spot?

Question 2—Which of the following best characterizes where you are in the journey to clarity:

- I'm uncertain and confused about my unique mission of good works and deeds.
- I'm not living in the sweet spot of my unique mission. I need to make a change and know the general direction I need to go.
- I'm generally living close to my unique mission, but need to make some tweaks to be more effective.
- I'm close to my sweet spot and just need affirmation.

Our Unique Mission (uM)

Similar to our unique identity (uI) in chapter 12, our unique mission (uM) is a succinct statement shaping the theme of our unique good works and deeds, ideally reflected in less than a sentence.

For example, Billy Graham was an evangelist of Christ Jesus (his core identity of BE) who called people to repentance and new life (core theme or purpose). An evangelist is one who recruits, proclaims, and tells. This unique identity could overflow into and express itself in thousands of different ways. Graham's unique mission expressed itself in proclaiming the good news of Jesus and calling people into a restored relationship with him. Graham's effectiveness in living out the purpose of his DO was amplified because it is an overflow of who he was created to BE.

Consider Paul, an apostle of Christ Jesus (his unique identity of BE) who planted the gospel message among the Gentiles. An apostle is like an entrepreneur. They start, extend, and scale things. Entrepreneurs can engage in thousands of different purposes. God gave Paul a unique mission to carry the gospel message to the Gentiles.

As we saw in the last chapter, I am an "entrepreneurial engineer of Christ Jesus." At my core I have the traits of an apostle or entrepreneur with a bias to problem solving and strategy. My unique mission (uM) is to "help leaders envisage future opportunities." To envisage is to create an image or picture of a future possibility.

After years of helping others discern their unique good works and deeds, I've found three questions that help people gain clarity on their unique mission (uM):

1. What are my natural talents and abilities?
2. What am I most passionate about?
3. What am I most burdened by?

171

Put your investigator hat on. Your life is the story holding all the clues. Engage intentionally in discerning the answers to these questions. Armed with this understanding and clarity, you can then look at how the integration of your answers can most effectively express themselves in harmony and overflow from who you were uniquely created to be (from chapter 12).

Consider this simple analogy. You are baking something using a recipe. The ingredients are on the counter and include sugar, water, and flour. These ingredients are analogous to your unique traits of gifting, passions, and burdens. What are you baking? Sugar, water, and flour can create thousands of different baked goods. You need to know more ingredients to discern what the recipe produces. Let's add vanilla, chocolate chips, and a dash of salt. Now it sounds a lot like chocolate chip cookies. The more we know about the basic ingredients, the better we can discern what they are designed to produce. The same is true of our unique mission (uM).

Good Works

DO

Characteristics revealing what I'm made to do!

Spend the time necessary to understand and discern your unique ingredients of talents, passions, and burdens. They are not accidental. God knew what he was doing when he formed you in your mother's womb. Those unique ingredients are part of a unique recipe authored by God.

This lens is similar to previous ones. Each line protruding from the center "DO" of the lens represents the basic ingredients or characteristics that shape your unique mission (uM). As you work through the exercises and the questions below, add the appropriate words to the "lens."

Diane got her college degree in chemistry and enjoyed her job as a technician in a cancer research laboratory. When children came along, she felt a strong conviction to be a stay-at-home mother. For sixteen years she put her professional career on hold. The kids have now graduated, her credentials and training feel outdated, and she is left wondering what to do next. She is wrestling to discover her unique mission (uM).

As you read through the questions below, notice how Diane's unique mission (uM) reveals itself. Consider how the "clues" shape and inform her unique purpose. Take the time to work through the exercise for yourself. Visit www. personalcalling.org to see additional examples of this exercise in action.

WHAT ARE MY NATURAL TALENTS AND ABILITIES?

Natural talents and abilities are those things we are naturally good at and can easily be translated into skills and competencies. StrengthsFinder (from chapter 12) is a good source. Brainstorm a list of as many talents as you can think of that seem to "follow you" wherever you go across all domains of life. These are things that seem to come naturally to you and are often affirmed by others. Consider surveying friends, family members, and coworkers to get their input on identifying your top strengths.

Diane, our stay-at-home mom who is reentering the workforce after sixteen years, found the following descriptive words through her StrengthsFinder profile:

- *Harmony* (building consensus, avoiding conflict)
- *Responsibility* (being reliable in doing what she commits to)
- *Maximizer* (naturally sees weaknesses and opportunities for improvement)
- *Deliberative* (careful in decision making)
- *Connectedness* (sees the links between things)

While Diane is not charismatic, inspirational, or entrepreneurial, she is loyal and reliable. Her strengths make her a great leader of teams that are responsible for maintaining consistently high standards.

WHAT ARE MY PASSIONS?

Passions are the things that naturally give us energy and life and charge our batteries. We'd spend as much of our time as possible doing these types of things if money and family commitments were not limiting us. In reflecting on the passions that have energized Diane during the recent years at home with the kids, she highlights the following:

- Playing a supportive role in helping others
- Being part of something important that is bigger than me
- Doing things with excellence and integrity
- Truth, freedom, and liberty; personal rights and opportunity

Some key words for Diane include: *supporting*, *helping*, *significance*, *excellence*, *truth*, and *liberty*.

What Are My Burdens/Convictions?

Burdens and convictions weigh on our heart and shape our thinking. Most people have a hard time putting their finger on burdens. You will likely need to look harder at your "I remember when . . ." list, and you may need to commit for a season of time to prayerfully listen for clues. The Holy Spirit whispers the clues. Diane is burdened/convicted by:

- The downward spiral of our culture and values
- Education and the decline of our young people's ability to think critically
- Stewardship of her time and talent
- The impact of illegal immigration

WHAT ARE KEY CHARACTERISTICS OF MY UNIQUE DESIGN/CORE IDENTITY?

In reflecting on the characteristics of her core identity (cI) from chapter 12, Diane concluded: "I am an Operational Team Leader." Key traits include:

- Responsibility
- Harmony
- Maximizer
- Consistency
- Developer of people

Integration

Diane might write the following as her first attempt at a unique mission: "My unique mission is to help instill the importance and value of education, lifelong learning, and critical thinking into our next generation of young leaders."

Diane's understanding of her unique mission will continue to evolve and clarify with time. The key question for Diane, as for most people, is where to position herself to best accomplish this purpose (the focus of GO in chapter 14).

As you complete the questions above and continue to think through these elements of your unique mission (uM) of DO, look for core themes and patterns. You are assembling the puzzle pieces, one at a time. Don't worry about choosing the perfect phrase initially. For now, simply write down in one sentence a statement of your unique mission (uM) based on your answers to the questions above.

A few years ago, my level of clarity was simply "equipping leaders." That's not very specific. With time, my talents and passions have come into increasing clarity around a core mission of "helping people create an image of future opportunities and a strategy for implementing them." The same will happen for you. Don't worry if your first attempt at this lens yields a vague or general purpose. Trust the process to become increasingly more specific with time as you discover and assemble more clues.

Whatever You Do . . .

In his letter to the Colossians, Paul said, "Whatever you do, whether in word or deed, do it all in the name of the Lord

Jesus" (3:17). He also said later in that chapter, "Whatever you do, work at it with all your heart, as working for the Lord. . . . It is the Lord Christ you are serving" (3:23–24). Paul had little to say about our specific purposes, but lots to say about why and how we do whatever we do.

As we search out our calling, remember Jesus is at the center of everything. Our calling starts with Jesus, is about Jesus, is for Jesus, and is to lead people to Jesus. Our general calling is to make the name and person of Jesus more famous.

Let us always remember the purpose of our unique DO is found in him alone!

Calling is found where we are and where we are meant to be. In the following chapter we take a deeper look at the question, "Where is my unique position (uP) for living out the mission God has placed in my life?"

Visit www.personalcalling.org for supplemental resources.

CHAPTER 14

Where I'm Most Effective: My Unique Position

Then I heard the voice of the Lord saying,
"Whom shall I send? And who will go for us?"
And I said, "Here am I. Send me!"
He said, "Go and tell this people . . ."

ISAIAH 6:8–9A

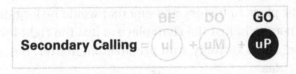

Secondary Calling. Where should I GO to be most effective? What is my unique position (uP)?

I'm not a gifted athlete nor am I a passionate sports fan. I am, however, intrigued by the characteristics that distinguish great teams from merely good teams.

It was my freshman year at North Carolina State University. Our men's basketball team, the Wolfpack, was playing at home. The game is memorable not just because my wife, Anna, and I made it our first date, but also because it marked the start of a historic journey for the Wolfpack from mediocrity to greatness, culminating in a national basketball championship.

The scrappy Wolfpack team found a way to win games down the stretch regardless of the odds. They won seven of their final games by coming from behind in the last minute. It was electric as momentum built. To further dramatize this epic journey, the championship game against a heavily favored opponent came down to the final shot.

Derek Whittenburg threw up a desperate, poorly executed thirty-foot air ball as the final seconds ticked down. No worries. His teammate Lorenzo Charles was perfectly positioned to jump, grab the ball, and complete a slam dunk as the final second ticked to zero.

Ball. Hoop. Horrendous shot. Unexpected dunk. National championship.

Reflect on the magic of this moment. Months of practice, an entire season with over twenty-five games, a conference underdog championship to land a position in the post-season tournament, and now the final forty minutes to determine the national champion. It all came down to one final second. In that moment of destiny, the difference between a team that would mark their place in history and one that would be forgotten was one person in just the right place at just the right time!

Talent, skill, strategy, and preparation matter, but position rules.

Both of my boys played youth soccer. If you've ever watched young kids play during their first season, they are like ants and the ball is like food. All the players from both teams swarm on the ball as it moves up and down the field. It's a junior version of "king of the hill" as everyone pursues the glory that comes with first getting the ball and then scoring. We instinctively know that the hero must have the ball to score, so we race toward it, not recognizing our place of impact might be away from the ball.

After a few seasons, my youngest son found himself on a winning team. For two straight seasons they never lost a game, but not because they were stacked with superstar athletes.

I asked their coach about the secret to their success. He said, "It's quite easy. I teach them the principle of position." He went on to explain that a kid's natural bias is to go where the ball is. He said, "I teach them to always know where the ball is, to know where the goal is, but to then discern where they should best position themselves to support getting the ball into the other team's goal or keeping it away from their own goal. The principle of position requires them to anticipate the future and learn to position themselves accordingly."

Yes, talent and good plays are important, but consistently positioning yourself in the right place to support the overall mission is what distinguishes the great teams from those that are merely good. The same is true for you and me in the sport of calling. We can perfectly understand our unique identity (uI) and design (BE) and have crystal clarity on our unique mission (uM) of good works and deeds (DO) but still be poor stewards of our calling. The principle of position—where we engage to be the most effective steward (GO)—makes all the difference.

This instinctively makes sense for most of us, and yet unique position is the element of calling that is most confusing and difficult for many people to discover. This is in part because we are conditioned to accept what's available rather than find what's best. When we enter a parking lot, we look for the best open spot. We take what we can get. When waiting at a restaurant, we take the next empty table. When we graduate from high school or college, we find the best job available, not necessarily the job that lines up with our unique personal calling.

Too often we allow the tensions and circumstances of life, including making a living, to constrain our calling rather than allowing calling to shape our lives. As we look deeper into this final dimension of personal calling, remember that finding the position where you can be most effective produces a much different outcome than merely accepting what is available.

The Context for GO

In our general or primary calling shared with all Christians, everywhere, all the time, we are called to be disciples who make disciples where we are. Recall from chapter 11 that "where I am" is our core mission field for carrying the fullness of Jesus to the world. From our workplaces to our children's sports teams to the health club, most of us already have more than fifty relationships of influence. If we are candid, most of us don't need to physically move or go somewhere else to have a ripe mission field for making disciples.

God may call us to pack our bags and go to a new geographic location as he did Abraham. That new location will simply provide a new mission field for being a disciple who makes disciples. Our first point of stewardship is to be an intentional disciple maker and good steward of the mission field God has already entrusted to our care. GO might mean repositioning ourselves to be more effective where we already are.

For most people reading this book, the mission field we already find ourselves in is the best place to start in putting our unique BE-DO into action. We start by envisioning what we already have . . . differently and with new eyes. We are to engage and deploy our unique calling where we can be most effective (the subject of this chapter), but we are to begin where we are. Sometimes our GO requires a move; other times it doesn't.

The GO or position element of calling helps bring the BE and DO elements to life within a specific context. Think of the progression of BE-DO-GO (uniquely made—unique good works—unique position) as a funnel that narrows down to a more focused output.

For example, the apostle Paul is uniquely created to BE an apostle or pioneer. Recall that apostles start, extend, scale, and grow new things. Paul was uniquely called to proclaim and plant the gospel message as he started new churches (his DO). Where did he uniquely GO? To the Gentiles. And even further, the Holy Spirit directed him with the vision of the man from Macedonia (Acts 16:9), showing him exactly where he needed to go next. Paul's unique calling of BE-DO-GO was to be an apostle of Christ Jesus who carried the gospel message to the Gentiles. Most of us reading this book now can trace our spiritual roots to Paul's personal calling. It was his GO that brought the gospel message to us.

For Paul, notice how his GO "to the Gentiles" significantly narrows down and brings focus to his BE-DO calling to "be an apostle of Jesus who proclaimed and planted the gospel." His unique BE-DO elements of calling could have been lived out in thousands of unique GO contexts. Our core position (cP) is the cause, outcome, role, organization and/or physical location where we can be the best possible stewards of the unique identity (cI) and unique mission (uM) God has placed in our lives.

Rethinking Position

"GO" and "position" are often synonymous with a physical place or geography. When Lorenzo Charles scored that game-winning shot, it was his physical location that made all the difference. Some people are called to serve in a geographic location or specific strategic context. For example, missionaries like my friend Alan Hirsch are called to geographic places where they can use their unique gifts, passions, and burdens.

However, GO is not always a physical place. The apostle Paul was actually called to a people group, which in turn took him to specific places. In a similar way, we might be called to serve single mothers, mentally challenged children, or people with a specific cancer. These are all examples of a GO or position that finds its sweet spot in serving a specific group of people. The physical place becomes important only in the

181

context of being strategic in reaching the cause or people we are called to.

Others are called to a specific cause or desired outcome. Their GO might be "the race to cure breast cancer" or the "opportunity to eliminate homelessness in a city" or "the mission to eliminate leprosy among a certain people group." The examples are endless. My unique calling is rooted in a desired outcome: My GO is anywhere there are "opportunities with significant potential for kingdom impact." This transcends specific causes, people groups, and physical locations.

Our GO can be any combination of physical location, people group, cause, or outcome. Your GO may be rooted in just one or in some combination of these.

Our BE and DO stay with us over time. Yet our GO often changes throughout life. Picture a charter fishing boat. While its unique design and purpose remain unchanged throughout its life, its rudder can take it to many different places. Similarly, our unique BE and DO remain consistent, but our unique GO is like the rudder on a boat with the potential to take us consistently to one place or to many different places.

In Search of Compatibility

As we pursue our unique position (uP) of GO, there are three changes we may need to consider.

First, do we stay where we are, working within the same company or context, but make an adjustment to create a more aligned fit? We may simply need a new role or project within our current company or a new emphasis in our free time. This is the least disruptive change. A slight repositioning can make all the difference. As noted above, we may simply need to see the opportunities in our current mission field differently.

Second, it may be impossible within our current context to get an alignment of our BE-DO-GO. Often this occurs when an organization or position's values, rhythms, and roles simply cannot be compatible with us. Our personal values may be different than the organization's, or the job requirements and demands may be inconsistent with our natural life rhythms, or the "best fit" roles may simply not be available inside the organization. We may need to change our place of employment. Often this requires a change in organizations, but not necessarily uprooting and moving our families.

Finally, we may receive a word from God as Abraham did to pack our bags and go, or we may need to follow our passions to physically move to a new location. This is obviously the most intrusive of changes. Remember, our GO creates the unique context for our local mission field. Be cautious and seek counsel here. Because of the disruptive impact of moving, we should be confident that it's a call from God and not just the hope the "grass will be greener on the other side of the fence."

For most people, the financial realities of providing for our families and ourselves provide a filter through which we address the potentially disruptive ramifications of our actions. Will there be seasons when we have no option but to live with our unique BE-DO-GO out of alignment? Yes. Do we need to accept that as a permanent reality? No. At a minimum we should work to maximize the alignment within the current constraints of our lives.

This may mean making adjustments in our current vocation and role as we wait for the right timing on more disruptive changes (such as switching companies or moving). This can also include becoming better stewards of our time outside our paid vocation. What does it look like to maximize the alignment of our unique BE-DO-GO in our families and our nonvocational time where we have more control?

Regardless of our unique position (uP), we can seek to improve our "fit" where we already are. Optimizing our current "fit" is about compatibility. In coaching people in discovering their unique fit, three questions prove helpful and are a good place to start:

1. What are my *personal values* and are they compatible with my organization?
2. What are the current and upcoming realities of the *rhythms of my life*, and are they compatible with my role?
3. What are the *natural types of roles* that are most compatible with my unique wiring, and am I currently in one of them?

The following sections address each of these three elements in more detail.

PERSONAL VALUES

Personal values shape how we do everything we do. They are always present like a magnetic force field, shaping and influencing everything that comes in their path. As I write this I'm visiting Disney World. It's been nearly fifty years since Walt Disney's death and yet his values live on through his parks. As we walk around, we experience Disney's personal value of cleanliness, a concept so deeply engrained in the organization that it penetrates and shapes everything.

Don't underestimate the power of personal values and their impact on our unique BE-DO-GO. Our unique personal values are part of our design from God. My unique GO of "wherever there is significant potential for kingdom impact" links directly to my personal values of multiplication, stewardship, results, and the local church. In a similar way, I've found that many people who have strong personal values linked to justice and compassion are passionate about social justice issues and find their unique GO rooted in causes.

There is often a gap between our personal values and the cultural values we experience in the organizations we work within. The larger the gap, the more frustration we experience. The smaller the gap, the more joy we feel in our work. Incompatibility of values is one of the biggest undiagnosed causes of job dissatisfaction.

Although competency and character are critical, I've grown to appreciate the vital importance of ensuring that an employee's personal values align with the organization's. Picture two horses pulling a stagecoach. What happens if they try to pull in opposite directions? Yet the reality is our personal values will only perfectly align with an organization if we are the founder and the organization remains small. All other scenarios will produce some degree of gap. We must learn to diagnose such gaps and position ourselves in compatible organizations.

John is a salesman in the medical services field. He values relationships and a caring environment. He finds himself increasingly frustrated and drained by the culture at work, complaining that his company puts financial results and performance above relationships. There is a gap between John's values and the organization's values. Relationships and a caring environment are great things. But so are strong performance and an excellence culture. Don't focus on which is better. Instead, focus on the gap. John may need to find a new company.

Personal values are so deeply rooted in who we are that we rarely pause to think about them. They are natural and instinctual. Unfortunately, most people are unable to articulate them. We become confused between what we'd like them to be (which is aspirational) and what they actually are (which is reality). Gaining clarity on our personal values is vital to gaining clarity on our unique personal calling.

RHYTHMS AND CONSTRAINTS OF LIFE

Consider a life of complete freedom. No debt, no money worries, and no commitments constraining your decisions. No concerns or obstacles to limit you from living out your unique calling. In an ideal world, we'd build the rhythm of life around our unique BE-DO-GO calling. Or, said differently, we'd orient the activities of life around our calling. We'd be free to do anything and go anywhere as we live it out.

Realistically, most of us don't have this flexibility. We live in the real world with real constraints. Furthermore, the realities of life—including our family commitments, work responsibilities, community commitments, relationships, and other demands of our time, talent, and treasure—shape and define our unique mission field or position. It's a paradox of sorts.

It's helpful to change our paradigm and embrace the rhythms and demands of life as a positive thing. We need to build the realities of our rhythms of life into our unique position (uP) of GO. Our commitments and constraints often create the context for the relationships we have access to and the mission field where we are. In these very relationships we have the ability to carry the fullness of Jesus as we seek to fulfill our general calling of making disciples.

Consider Susan, a professional working mother who is the deputy mayor of a large city. Her unique identity and mission made her the ideal candidate for the position. However, she struggled with accepting the role. Susan wanted to be home each day at 3 p.m. when the kids arrived from school. Susan was firm in her commitment to her children and successfully navigated a creative solution. She negotiated a role that allowed her to be home with her children from 3 p.m. to 7 p.m. each day, instead working occasional evenings and weekends.

Examples of the rhythms-of-life constraints we should consider include:

Financial requirements to provide for family. We may need to change our lifestyle and live more frugal lives to create margin for increased engagement of our unique calling, either vocationally or in our volunteer roles. For most of us, financial realities will at least partially shape our GO. Be realistic and define these rhythms.

Time commitments. There are many demands on our time including work, volunteer roles, kids' sports, and so on. Like our finances, we can partially control these things. However, there should and will be specific commitments that are non-negotiable and built into the rhythm of our GO.

Work commitments. Most of us spend more than half of our waking hours engaged in our vocational jobs. While we can change jobs or renegotiate requirements, we must honor our existing commitments.

Family needs. Our family needs the best of us. Discipling our spouses and children, and providing for their physical, spiritual, and emotional needs is of utmost importance. We should be realistic in spending quality time with them. Where possible, look for family rhythms that can overlap with your GO.

Personal health and spiritual priorities. Maintaining both our physical and spiritual health should be a daily priority. Sleep, healthy meals, exercise, and time in Bible reading, prayer, and corporate worship are all necessary to keep us in the best shape to live out our personal calling.

Living in our sweet spot does require sacrifice and surrender. You may need to prune things from your life. At the same time, you must be very clear about your non-negotiable priorities and build those into the rhythm of your unique position of GO.

NATURAL ROLES

The world needs all kinds of people for all kinds of roles. We each have a natural affinity to certain types of roles and influence. Some of us are wired to be technicians, spending our entire careers being responsible for a concrete and well-defined set of responsibilities. Others are wired to be supervisors and team leaders, while some are made to lead entire corporations.

I've found it useful to think about natural roles through two different dimensions. The first comes directly from a construct used by the Paterson Center (www.patersoncenter.com) called "Thinking Wavelength." The tool has people self-select into one of five different natural roles of influence. As you read the following descriptions, which one best reflects your natural bias? The question is not "what can I do" but rather "what type of role do I most naturally have an affinity to?" Don't be distracted by the labels. The substance of the characteristics behind the labels is what's most important.

"Grinders"—people who naturally enjoy and influence the outcome through direct, concrete, tasks and thinking. These people tend to be risk averse and thrive on producing results in a structured, well-defined work environment. Grinders faithfully and reliably get the work of the organization done, and they find their joy in contributing to the overall outcome.

"Minders"—Like Grinders, these people like tangible, hands-on work, but they also enjoy the increased responsibilities characteristic of supervisors. These people are often selected for positions of increased responsibility, including management and supervision. These people enjoy getting involved not just with getting work done, but also in how it is organized and more efficiently executed. These people naturally assume ownership not just for their unique role, but for how the overall job, people, and tasks integrate together.

"Builders"—These people prefer to oversee a broader scope of tasks and functions. They often serve as middle-level managers, supervisors, or team leaders in positions of influence over people and processes. They are often good with planning, strategy, and seeing how the vision translates to the work that needs to be done. They see both the big picture and the micro and have a knack for prioritizing and scheduling work to meet budgets and schedules.

"Finders"—These people are the entrepreneurs and leaders who start, grow, and run organizations. They are naturally drawn into vision, values, and strategy, especially as they relate to accomplishing the mission. They often find themselves in charge without really trying. CEOs and senior leaders are typically Finders.

"Conceivers"—These people are full of ideas and theories. They live in their heads, which never seem to shut off from coming up with new ideas (regardless of their practicality). Conceivers dream up the ideas that "finders" seize and take to fruition.

PREFERRED WORK ENVIRONMENT

A second vantage point for looking at our natural roles involves the environment that we prefer to work within. Here are some questions to consider:

- Are you naturally a "lone ranger" preferring to work independently or a "team member" preferring a more collaborative environment?
- Do you prefer to be the boss or a subordinate?
- Do you prefer to be a decision maker or an advisor to others who make decisions?
- Do you naturally find yourself in positions of leadership or do you prefer to stay in less visible roles?
- Do you prefer a work environment that is intense and demanding or relaxed and flexible?
- Do you prefer a work environment that is fast and aggressive or slow and methodical?
- Do you prefer a work environment that has lots of variability and change or predictability and stability?
- Do you prefer freedom and autonomy or structure and order?

Consider John, an architect in his own firm. His office assistant is his only employee. John is a "Minder" on the "Thinking Wavelength" and has no desire to build a firm that requires additional employees. He enjoys doing the core architectural work himself and does not like the headaches of managing people. John is a "lone ranger" who prefers to make decisions himself. He prefers a relaxed and flexible work environment (e.g., home office) that is slow, methodical, predictable, and stable. John prefers freedom and autonomy. A small, hands-on firm like the one John founded is perfect for him.

Application: Finding My Unique Position (uP)

The following exercise will help you move toward clarity in your unique GO. Visit www.personalcalling.org to download a self-guided worksheet for completing the following exercise. This guide also includes examples of how other people have completed this exercise.

Step 1—Look back at the passions and burdens you identified in the last chapter. Identify any that could shape or influence your unique GO.

Step 2—Seek to identify at least five personal values that shape how you do most everything you do. For example, you may value frugality and thrift. The frugality gene is embedded within your DNA. What values are always with you?

Step 3—Seek to identify several rhythms-of-life constraints that must be considered in assessing your current and future roles.

Step 4—Write a short description of the type of role that most naturally fits your unique design and wiring using the Paterson Center framework of Grinder, Minder, Builder, Finder, and Conceiver. Add additional characteristics and descriptive words as applicable.

Step 5—Use the list of questions under "Preferred Work Environment" (page 189) to characterize the type of role you most naturally fit. Select the descriptor that best describes you in each question.

Step 6—Write down a rough draft or statement of your unique BE-DO (unique core design and unique core mission) from chapters 12 and 13. It can be a sentence, paragraph, or simply a few words from your reflections in previous chapters. Keep it simple and succinct.

Step 7—You've likely had a number of different full-and part-time jobs. You've probably also volunteered in various organizations. Any role you've had involving people and tasks holds clues to your unique fit. From cub scout den leader to team mom, every role gives more insights. Create a list of all the jobs/roles you've had in your career, including part-time and different roles within the same company, as well as volunteer roles.

Step 8—Using the list you created in Step 7, answer the following questions using a ranking system, with 1 meaning "not at all" and 5 meaning "completely."

- Did the responsibilities of the role strongly *align with and overflow* from my unique BE-DO?
- Did the organization's values strongly align with my *personal values*? Which ones aligned and which ones did not?
- Did the position empower me in *unique roles* that fit my natural wiring?
- Did the role accommodate my *unique personal rhythms and constraints*?
- Did the role genuinely give me *joy* amidst the toil of work? Did I enjoy work and look forward to going each day?
- Did the position naturally help me be a good *steward* of the time, talent, and treasure God entrusts to my care by creating ongoing *opportunities* that have led to meaningful *impact*?
- Did the role help me to be more effective in my local *mission field* as a disciple who makes disciples where I am (the GO from my general calling in chapter 11)?

The downloadable supplementary resources at www. personalcalling.org will help you probe into these questions more deeply and give examples of how the questions are applied. You can also apply these questions to future opportunities to assess your compatibility for that role.

Step 9—As you assess each question, also reflect on the specific factors that cause you to give the rating that you do. For example, if you assign a "1" (not at all) as an answer, also write down what caused that low compatibility. Be specific. In a similar way, identify what makes a "5" so strongly compatible or a "3" only partially compatible. This assessment of gaps in your past roles is one of the best tools you have for discerning the factors that make you compatible (or incompatible) in a specific role or place. Your answers cut to the heart of personal values, life rhythms, and natural roles. Don't be surprised if some of the worst jobs you've had give you the best insights. We learn as well from misalignment as from alignment.

Step 10—Fill in the "Lens" diagram below (or create a list of characteristics). Each line extending from "GO" is a key word or phrase that describes you. Each personal value, natural role, and personal rhythm statement go on a line.

Position

GO

Where can I be most effective?

Step 11—Consider whether the words on your lens lend additional clarity to your unique BE-DO. Make any necessary adjustments to your BE-DO. For me, this process occurred over time. As I pressed into my unique position (uP) of GO, I gained further clarity in my BE-DO. Our personal values are strongly linked to our burdens and passions that are embedded in our unique mission (uM) of DO. You may need to refine the distinction between your DO and your GO as you gain more clarity through the years.

Step 12—Do an initial gut check to discern whether your unique GO is a physical location, a people group, a cause, a trigger/condition, an outcome, or some combination of all these elements. Take your first stab at writing down your unique GO. If necessary, include several different possibilities. Use this as your starting point for increased clarity in the future.

Step 13—Using what you've learned from the steps above, write a description of the "roughly right" role and work environment in which your unique BE-DO-GO would function most effectively. This step is not intended to identify a specific organization, but rather to highlight the characteristics that the ideal environment might look like.

A Final Thought

This process of discerning your unique position (uP) can seem overwhelming, but remember that God is on your side. At this point, you might even be thinking, "This is too good to be true; a perfect position that aligns with my unique values, rhythms, and wiring?" You might have your doubts, but let your skepticism dwell on the words of Ephesians 2:10 one more time: "For we are God's handiwork, created in Christ Jesus to do good works, which God prepared in advance for us to do."

The time and place of your birth were ordained. God knew your parents and early experiences before the world ever existed. Your wiring and need for the perfect fit are part of his plan for you. As you look for your unique position, trust the Author and Guide to show you amazing things. You'll find that God will open doors for you to be the right person at the right time in the right place.

Visit www.personalcalling.org for supplemental resources.

CHAPTER 15

The Importance of Mentors

> Follow my example, as I follow the example of Christ.
>
> 1 CORINTHIANS 11:1

Jesus didn't start a university.
He also didn't start a government or a corporation or a dynamic nonprofit to address issues of social justice. All of those entities are good things (or can be). All of them are needed for a functioning society. Yet when Jesus began the movement of the church, to share the most important mission the world has ever known, his primary approach was role modeling holiness and a Spirit-led life, coupled with investing in twelve close friends.

He taught the masses. He loved and spoke to and healed people that came across his path. But he deeply invested in a small group of people that he lived with and ate with, and these individuals shared years of his life. They were the standard bearers of the movement to come.

What a journey! Scripture indicates that Peter knew of Jesus a year before his call at Galilee. He had probably heard him speak. He had heard about healings and other miracles. He had been in conversations with Andrew about the possibility of Jesus being the Messiah. After Peter's call, he spent three years with Jesus, learning, watching, and asking questions. After the resurrection Jesus said, "Feed my sheep" (John 21:17) and prophesied how Peter's death would glorify God (John 21:19).

Then we see Peter in the book of Acts, and the race is on.

Look at the amazing transformation that occurred through the direct life-on-life coaching and accountability of his mentor, Jesus. Peter moves from "come and see" to "follow me" to "feed my sheep" to "die for me."

Think about the college student about to enter the job market, or the businesswoman about to launch her first entrepreneurial venture. Consider the stay-at-home parent with two college degrees, about to reenter a job market after a sixteen-year hiatus. Think about the grandparents about to retire from the corporate world but wanting a life filled with meaning and activity. They all need the same thing. They need a coach to help them and to speak into their lives, especially in times of transition. The power of a one-on-one coach or mentor simply cannot be overstated.

We see this one-on-one impact over and over again in life and in Scripture. Think of Elijah and Elisha, Samuel and David, Paul and Timothy, and Peter and Mark.

One-on-one coaching is a critical piece of our journey. It amplifies the discovery and effectiveness of calling.

My Most Regular Prayer

By far, my most frequent prayer in recent years for my sons has been, "Please put the right people, at the right time, in the path of my boys." As they transitioned from the care of parents to independence and the influence of the broader world, we knew the profound impact other people would have on them. The company we keep and the influences to which we submit shape who we become.

Each of us can pinpoint specific people who've had profound positive and negative influences on our lives. With little effort, I can compile a list of people beyond my immediate family members who've shaped my values, my thinking, my family, and my career.

Gordon Monson, a retired professional golfer, came alongside me, teaching me the finer points of golf. Bill Shirley took me under his wing at Naval Reactors, helping me to be a better engineer, leader, and manager. Brett Andrews encouraged me relentlessly to let go of the things keeping me from entering full-time ministry. Ron Ferguson was a wise, trusted friend who said, "You need to go into full-time ministry" at the height of my doubts. Troy McMahon provided a role model for transitioning from the corporate world to vocational ministry. Bob Buford catalyzes continuing clarity on my personal calling and sharpens my thinking on personal values. And this is just a quick list.

In most cases, the method of influence in my life has not been complex. It's an intersection of relationship with words I need to hear. It's an investment of time and a willingness to be teachable. Don't underestimate the importance of a few choice words, delivered at just the right time.

Several years ago I founded Exponential (www.exponential.org), which serves leaders who start new churches. Each year, at least one of our conference attendee comes to me and says something like, "Thank you. You have no idea the impact last year's conference had on me." The first time this happened I expected the person to give a profound reason involving the scope of programing: one hundred fifty speakers, two hundred workshops, and so on. To my surprise, nearly every person says something like, "I came ready to quit. When I heard [fill in the blank] say [fill in blank], it rocked my world. It changed the trajectory of my thinking and ministry."

I then find myself thinking, "Seriously? I don't remember the speaker even saying that. And even if he did, it doesn't seem that profound to me. One sentence or phrase from a person's mouth changes your trajectory? Really?" But it's true. I've found that these entrepreneurial leaders tend to be lonely and discouraged in their journey. They have tons of passion, vision, and dreams, but they are lacking in permission and encouragement. The power of another person coming alongside them, putting their arm around them, and saying, "You can do this. I believe in you" is all it takes to change one's course.

The words "You can do it" are profoundly powerful.

Key Influencers

In thinking of a way to express learnings and observations about coaching, I kept coming back to a key influencer in my own life, Bob Buford. Bob is the author of the best-selling book *Halftime* and founder of Leadership Network, and he entered my life about eighteen years ago. I was wrestling at a relatively young age with what I'd with the rest of my life. As I pondered my life, I was asking, should I stay in my career or should I go into ministry?

I stumbled onto Bob's newly released book *Halftime*, where he shares his own journey of moving beyond the success of his business career into the sweet spot of his calling. The message resonated with me and influenced my journey. Although I'd not met Bob, his journey of moving from success to significance stuck with me.

Fast-forward ten years. I'd left the job I loved in the marketplace for a new season of discovering and living in my sweet spot. I'd never met Bob when I literally ran into him, face-to-face, in Dallas, Texas, during a business trip. We sat down and talked for three full hours. From complete strangers to friends just like that. A camaraderie, chemistry, and shared values emerged almost immediately.

With passion during those first few hours of meeting, Bob shared example after example of principles Peter Drucker, the father of modern management (and author of over ninety books), had taught him. Peter had personally mentored Bob for over twenty-five years, and it was clear what a profound and lasting impact Peter had on Bob—lessons he was now naturally rubbing off on me. It was electric. The relationship between Peter and Bob is one of the best examples I've seen of a coaching relationship working incredibly well.

As our relationship developed over the subsequent years and Bob became a mentor for me as Peter had been for him, I grew to appreciate even more the profound impact of having a coach. Bob says on a regular basis, "You can do it; how can I help?" and "I want to do for others what Peter Drucker did for me." The cycle continues as I now want to do for others what Bob has done for me. A deep truth is that calling is intergenerational. We benefit from those who have gone before . . . and we invest in those to come.

Submit to the influence of a mentor and serve as a mentor for others. It's the way Jesus designed things to be.

Ask and the Door May Be Opened

You might be saying, "But I can't get a mentor like Peter Drucker." First, you probably don't need a Peter Drucker. What Peter did for Bob was far more important than who he was. The role the mentor plays trumps their fame or notoriety. Second, you might be surprised to learn that the mentors you think are out of reach are actually just an invitation away.

So how did Bob Buford get Peter Drucker as a mentor?

It began at the age of twenty-seven, when he engaged Peter, widely regarded as the most influential thinker in business and management in the last hundred years, for consulting with his broadcasting business. Bob had surveyed the landscape of business literature for wisdom, and found that most of the advice seemed faddish and shallow. In Peter, he discovered a soul mate, someone whose thinking seemed deeper and more solid, built upon timeless principles rather than merely following the current trend.

So he wrote a letter asking for a meeting. He put his letter through eight drafts before finally sending it, starting a relationship with Peter that turned out to be lifelong.

Consultation grew into friendship and a deep admiration, with Peter providing insight and counsel for Bob as a mentor throughout his life.

It all started with a simple letter asking for a meeting.

All mentorships start with a conversation and an invitation. Be bold. Sometimes we just need to ask!

Don't wait for the perfect mentor. Start where you are. Look for the people already in your life who know you. Possibly a friend or a coworker who has already walked a path you are starting down. Pick someone who will disciple you in the process.

Key Things a Mentor Does for Us

For over twenty years during Bob's transition away from the business world, Peter was an instrumental voice helping him discern and gain clarity on his personal calling. I interviewed Bob to more fully discover the core essence of what Peter gave him, and now what Bob seeks to give others. Here are some points he mentioned.

PERMISSION

Very early on, Peter challenged Bob that success wasn't just about money. It was about the positive impact that an entrepreneurial spirit can bring to real people of all stations. It was about being a pioneer and finding ways to share that inspiration with others.

In a letter to Bob after one of their meetings, Peter wrote these words: "The important thing is [not to give the money away, but] to put yourself to work and really make a difference. Find a few others in this field. What you are good at: the conceptual category. Your direction: to be an entrepreneur."

Look closely. You can see Bob's unique BE-DO-GO. This one short letter by his mentor and friend packed profound insights into Bob's sweet spot. We all need and are blessed by the accountability and insights of a coach or mentor.

Bob calls this dynamic in his own mentoring "giving permission." As he was making the transition in his own life from "success to significance," Peter was helping him see how his calling could play out. By nudging him with new ideas, Peter set Bob free to move from a wildly successful broadcasting career to an even more successful life. Those conversations and Peter's wisdom helped define the heart of Bob's principles in *Halftime* and the Leadership Network.

Peter was encouraging Bob to see his giftedness as so much more than making money. That his energy and perspective could be valuable outside of the business sphere. Then the next words came like thunder: "Find a few others in this field."

Can you see how this single note must have resonated with Bob? This tiny push of permission helped propel him into extending permission for thousands of others, ultimately impacting millions of people as "a few others" also found second-half significance in kingdom work!

Peter gave Bob permission to be who God created him to be.

ENCOURAGEMENT

In January 1989, Peter Drucker wrote to Bob Buford: "So you are pioneering, you are creating a new field of human activity almost. And you are setting standards of effectiveness. I've never seen anything as effective in such economy of means as Leadership Network, and I mean it. You're setting standards of responsibility."

Peter encouraged Bob to write the best-selling book *Halftime*. He worked with him through the Leadership Network to maximize the impact of megachurch leaders. Throughout their relationship there was encouragement to look at the bigger picture and to understand that Bob's impact would reach further than he imagined. Simple encouragement was a profound piece of the puzzle. To say "you can do it" and acknowledge the results that come carries a weight of significance in the coach/mentor role that is unmatched.

We can "borrow" the confidence of our mentor and step out onto uncertain ground. This kind of encouragement brings action to dreams and strength of heart to face undefined territory.

ACCOUNTABILITY

Bob mentioned that he was highly motivated to make progress on things he discussed with Peter before their next meeting. He didn't want to show up "empty handed," as it were. That rings true. If we have a mentor we admire, we have a strong motivation and bias to action where they are involved.

This can also be true in a mentoring relationship that is more focused.

Bob noticed that many people would engage a personal trainer for physical fitness and pay them for targeted coaching to help them reach their goals. One-on-one expertise and accountability is helpful for people trying to exercise and stay on track.

In typical Bob fashion, he took this "conceptual category" and applied it to his own context brilliantly. Bob has a love for literature. But his path of life hadn't allowed for a liberal arts degree, even though that might have been his personal preference. So, a bit later in life, he decided to engage a personal trainer in literature.

He contacted Dr. Larry Allums, a top expert in literature in the Dallas area. Bob invited Larry to walk with him through a study of the great books, meeting every other week. They would read Shakespeare, Marlowe, Homer, and then talk about what they had read for a couple of hours. By engaging an expert in the field, Bob had personal access to the very best in thinking and scholarship for each work they encountered.

For over thirteen years they've continued the relationship, moving through the classics and the great works of Western thought, to the topic of history, which is still ongoing.

This is fascinating for a few reasons. First, it's just a great idea. Is there something you want to pursue? Why not find an expert to help you pursue it? Second, there is an element of accountability and productivity that is helpful on a practical level.

Could Bob have acquired a reading list and done this on his own? Could he have found the books easily enough in any public library? Could Bob have found commentaries on Shakespeare and Homer without the assistance of Dr. Allums? Of course.

But working with a mentor sets up a different dynamic, doesn't it? With the specific time set aside, there is a deadline and a certain friendly pressure to keep things moving. Plus, there is the element of face-to-face, real interaction that is a critical element in the coaching/mentoring relationship. Bob has covered thousands of pages of the best literature ever written, with a mentor and friend to answer questions and to talk about the texts they've read, in an incredibly meaningful way.

Would he have covered the same ground, in the same way, without his personal trainer? That level of coaching and intentionality helped Bob amplify his learning. The coach/mentor relationship makes us more productive and effective in exactly this sort of way. It creates accountability for results.

FILLING VOIDS

In our interview Bob said that a mentor "fills a void in your life." He described losing his father at an early age and going through life as a "fatherless person." He then talked about men in his life that played that role to some extent and the incredible depth of meaning those relationships brought. The notion was that this kind of relationship brings something important that literally makes us more complete as people. He said it without saying it.

In many ways, Peter Drucker was a father to Bob Buford.

That kind of healing, that kind of mentoring, that kind of investment is one of the most profound activities we can participate in. Beyond the personal importance of our coaches and mentors, internally, the relationship facilitates real results. The divine appointment of Drucker and Buford continues to ripple through the next generation of our churches and our society at large.

What voids or needs in your life could a mentor help fill?

Your Spouse or Best Friend

When asked about the scope of lasting mentorship in his life, Bob highlighted three key people. The Holy Spirit, Peter Drucker, and his wife, Linda. On many occasions over the years, I've heard Bob say, "Linda thinks . . ." Rarely do we discuss an issue that affects Bob's life without him valuing Linda's perspective and insight. You might say, "When Linda speaks, Bob listens."

Look again at the list of things that the Holy Spirit does for us (see page 80) and at the things in this chapter that a mentor does for us. Our spouses and best friends naturally do many of these things.

Do you see your spouse and best friends as mentors? How does that change our interactions? Just as the Holy Spirit is a gift, our spouses and best friends are also an amazing resource.

Doing for Others

Jesus started a movement by coaching and mentoring a small group of followers. He embedded himself in them, influencing their values and thinking, and expecting them to do the same with others. Christianity is the most powerful movement in the history of the world. It has been perpetuated from generation to generation by Gospel-transformed individuals who in turn do for others what has previously been done for them.

Peter Drucker caught this vision. He once wrote: "My definition of success changed a long time ago. . . . Making a difference in a few lives is a worthy goal. Having enabled a few people to do the things they want to do: that's really what I want to be remembered for." As a result of his vision, Peter invested heavily in men like Bob. Bob Buford also caught the vision to pay that investment forward. He has an ongoing group of individuals that he mentors, seeking to speak into their lives in meaningful ways.

Bob talks frequently about doing for others what Peter did for him. He talks about investing in people in ways that set them free to be everything they were called by God to be. To invest in them in ways that help them find their sweet spot of calling.

As a mentor to me, Bob's influence leads me to go further in my own personal calling than I ever would have thought possible. His insights were a catalyst for this book. And his encouragement to write was invaluable.

Even now I find myself looking for other men to invest in. As I look at the landscape of my life and my own role in calling, I would say it this way: Now I want to do for others what Bob has done for me. And so the cycle continues. Mentoring works that way!

Visit www.personalcalling.org for supplemental resources.

CHAPTER 16

Living the Part

For we are God's handiwork, created in Christ
Jesus to do good works, which God prepared in
advance for us to do.

EPHESIANS 2:10

The Parable of the Talents is one of Jesus' teachings I'm inspired by and frequently drawn back to. I want to be a good steward of the calling God has on my life and the unique gifts he's given me.

In this parable, the stewards of two talents and five talents immediately put what they'd been given into action. The master praised both, saying, "Well done, good and faithful servant" (Matthew 25:21). The only steward who was called "wicked and lazy" (v. 26) was the one who failed to put what had been entrusted to him into action.

God cares more about what we do with what is given us than about the specific gift given. A gift left unopened dishonors the giver. In this parable, the talent could have been money, gold, land, or anything of value. The talent is an equipping by the master to accomplish his purposes. That can only happen when the talent is put into action.

We must "live the part" we've uniquely been given. The life of calling is a life of adventure. It is a place where risk is rewarded. It is a journey and a stewardship biased toward action.

We actually have the ability to be the love and the fullness of Christ in everything and in every way. Our start-up capital account is fully funded—so much so that we can afford to be incredibly generous.

We must see the primary or general calling we have to be disciples who make disciples expressing itself through our secondary or unique personal calling. We're called to multiply and work with the gifts God has already given us. Calling is the means we employ to turn one into two, two into four, and five into ten. It is our internal framework for uniquely putting love into action.

I want to see at least the doubling described in this parable in my life. In fact, I want to be the "good soil" in the parable of the sower that sees upwards toward a hundredfold return! We shouldn't separate God's promise that we can live life to the fullest measure from an expectation that we can experience a thirty, sixty, or even hundredfold return in our journey. Being a good steward of what he's uniquely given us to work with is connected to one day hearing him say, "Well done, good and faithful servant."

Let that linger. What does it truly mean for you to be a good steward of the unique calling God has given you?

Don't let fear, pleasure seeking, desire for security, or issues of character paralyze you. Be ruthless with anything in life that could steal your "well done" away.

One Stone or an Arsenal

I'm inspired by the story of David and Goliath. I want David's faith. I want to be fearless and undaunted for God. I want to go into battle with little more than a few stones and conquer giants in the name of Jesus.

The good news is we are equipped with exactly what we need to accomplish God's purposes for us. David only needed a sling and a stone. He did not need a strategic plan, margin in his life, or permission. All he needed was the experience already embedded in the story of his life—the skill of a shepherd boy and his sling—and a faith that would move his hands and feet into action.

Unfortunately, in our sinful nature, we carry doubts. The evil one uses those doubts to slow us down and even waylay us. God has an amazing script and part for us to play, but we can't let the evil one hijack it.

While the story of David and Goliath is about epic faith, don't miss the little bit of doubt that David might have carried with him. It's easy to miss amidst this inspirational story. We read, "Then he took his staff in his hand, chose five smooth stones from the stream, put them in the pouch of his shepherd's bag and, with his sling in his hand, approached the Philistine" (1 Samuel 17:40).

How many stones did David need? Look closely. He picked up five but only needed one. So why did he pick up five? Why not ten or fifteen? Why not taunt Goliath by holding up one stone and saying, "This is all I need to bring you down!" Could the voice in David's head possibly have said something like, "If I miss, I'll need another. I don't need more than five because if I miss that many times I will probably be dead."

It's our nature to plan and await clarity before we act. God wants us to see the "Goliath" opportunities in front of us and act now. Not in several years when we have more clarity, more margin, more strategy, and a more attractive opportunity. Instead he wants us to lean into what's directly in front of us and act with more faith.

That starts with putting more urgency on the opportunity of today! Pick up and use the one stone that is already in your hand.

What's Important Now?

I've mentioned it before, but several years ago I went through the formal process of looking at my unique personal calling with my friend Pete Richardson, a master Life Planner with the Paterson Center. We painstakingly went through the narrative of my life, outlining early years, school, career paths, and relationships in great detail. It was interesting to look back in this way, to remember deeply, and to again experience the emotions and lessons of shaping moments. It was an incredibly intense process.

Patterns started to emerge, along with a greater sense of clarity. In my own journey I had already made the leap from vocational nuclear engineer to vocational entrepreneurial kingdom engineer, and the Life Plan affirmed my decision and direction. The greater sense of clarity wasn't wisdom for a fork in the road, sensing which way to go. Instead it was a call to greater urgency. To do what God wanted me to do, I needed to narrow my focus. I needed to remove clutter from my life. I needed to become more intentional in specific things. Doing things the same way wasn't an option, and I deeply felt the weight of where I needed to go generally.

On the last hour of the last day, Pete took out a large sheet of paper. He wrote down the date and my age. Then he wrote a second date, three years into the future, and put my future age next to it.

Then he asked me to dream.

"What would your life look like if God blessed your newfound focus and intentionality? Where would you hope to be?" We set out a simple bullet list of descriptors, and they formed a target. Then he took out a fresh page for each bullet and titled it, "What's Important Now?" And I had to get practical. For each one, I needed to list a handful of specific things to accomplish in the next three to six months to establish momentum. These initial actions would set me on a course toward the three-year picture.

Those actions became my marching orders. It's one thing to see what could happen and be inspired. This occurs to us all the time. We go to a conference, read a great book, or hear an amazing story, and we think, "Yes—that's exactly it! That's where I need to go!"

LIVING THE PART

It's an entirely different thing to make a list of activities for the next three months to effect the changes we want to see, and then to follow through. Remember that the journey of calling is as much about the discipline of taking new steps day to day as it is about the moment of inspiration when the lightning strikes.

Force yourself right now to create a general picture or description of what "well done" could look like in three years. Then list specifically and concretely three to five things you *must do* in the next three months to give you momentum toward that three-year vision. Sling. Stone. Faith. Giant.

Moving Forward

Throughout this book we've looked at surrendering the leading role in our story. We've looked at stepping forward in faith, making progress in the fog. We've walked through the heart of calling—embracing the centrality of the gospel and the fullness of Jesus in us, and then allowing that fullness to overflow through us to the world around us. We've talked about the balancing act of deeply committing to a faith community and taking ownership for our proxy rather than delegating it away to others.

We've talked about the BE-DO-GO from Ephesians 2:10, which is the framework of what we're working toward, and about the joy found in the sweet spot of calling that goes deeper than circumstance or suffering or a cultural definition of success.

And finally, we've talked about the elements of primary and secondary calling and how the overflow of the love of God in us is unique, prepared before the beginning of the world for our context and place in his story.

You now have a decision to make. Will you live the part God has designed for you? Will you take actions now to put what we've learned into practice? Will you be a vibrant part of what God is doing in our generation?

If your answer is yes, then as your friend and collaborator in this process, I'm going to make two requests of you.

First, I'm asking you to *dream*.

What would your life look like three years from now if you fully embraced the path God is calling you to walk? Be specific and write down the thoughts in your heart of hearts. Set false modesty and cultural expectations of success aside for a moment. Imagine a blue sky and no budget limitations. Who would you be, if you could be your best self? What would you do, if you could do anything?

Second, I'm asking you to *follow through*.

Don't let the ideas of this book sit unused. Follow through in specific ways toward a life filled with *more* of the good things God wants you to walk in. As an engineer, I love process and practicality—so here are specific ways you can make the most of God's truth about calling as we've engaged it here.

1. THE TEN TRUTHS OF CALLING

Put the ten truths we've outlined in this book into your own words. Make them personal for you, and then put them in a place where you'll see them and remember them as you walk through life day to day. Below is the generic list. Make them personal (see the example in my dashboard section below).

Clarity of calling emerges when we learn to:

1. Trust deeply the author of our story.
2. Step forward in faith, even when we cannot see clearly.
3. Abandon the earthbound kingdom of me in order to gladly serve in the eternal kingdom of God.
4. Submit to the lordship of Jesus.
5. Embrace our mission to carry the fullness of Jesus to every corner of society.
6. Live in common with a healthy, local community of faith.
7. Take personal responsibility of the unique role Jesus gives us.
8. Trust the guidance and power of the Holy Spirit.

9. Be disciples of Jesus who make disciples where we are.
10. Fulfill our unique personal calling to play our role in God's mission where we can be most effective.

2. COMPLETE THE LENSES

In chapters 9–14 we talked about specific lenses of calling. If you haven't already, go through and do the exercises as a time of prayer and spiritual meditation. Let the Holy Spirit speak to you as you press into your calling. Seek to create a first draft of your answers in the dashboard below. Don't worry about getting exactly the right words. This is your starting point.

3. CREATE A DASHBOARD

Clarity of purpose in calling will emerge over time, and the reality is we'll spend the rest of our lives pursuing what calling truly means for each of us. Still, a starting point is good and real progress can be made! As an example, here is mine. This isn't final or finished, but is my best understanding of my role and calling as this point in the journey.

Your Dashboard

Truths I will embrace as I pursue my unique personal calling . . . (customize the following as appropriate for you)

I will trust deeply that God, the author of my story, has written a unique script for me;

I will step forward in faith, even when I can't see clearly;

I will seek daily to surrender the "kingship of me" for the lordship of Jesus;

I will embrace God's primary mission for me to carry the fullness of Jesus to every corner of society;

I will devote myself to living in common as a family member in a healthy, local community of faith;

I will take responsibility for the unique personal calling and role God has given me within my family of faith;

I will continually strive to submit to the guidance and
power of Holy Spirit, trusting him to reveal the
unique clues of my personal calling;

I will be a disciple of Jesus seeking to become more
filled with his fullness, allowing that fullness to
overflow to others as I seek to make disciples
wherever I am;

I will be a good steward of God's unique identity (uI)
and mission (uM) in my life, wherever I can be
most effective.

Customize each of the six elements below to reflect your
primary and secondary calling:

	BE	DO	GO
	My Core Identity (cI)	*My Core Mission (cM)*	*My Core Position (cP)*
Primary or General Calling	I am a disciple of Jesus, seeking to have his fullness maturing in me	who carries Jesus' fullness to others, making disciples	where I am!
	BE **Uniquely Made** IDENTITY/ DESIGN	**DO** **Purpose** MISSION/PURPOSE	**GO** **Position** MISSION FIELD/POSITION
Secondary or Unique Personal Calling			
	My Unique Identity (uI)	*My Unique Mission (uM)*	*My Unique Position (uP)*

4. FIND A COACH OR MENTOR

Look for someone who can speak permission, encouragement, and accountability into your life. Don't be discouraged if your first choice says no; they may be in a season of life where they aren't able to take on additional activity. Keep trying. Be proactive, be regular, and be specific. Allow your mentor to speak into your life!

5. BE SPECIFIC AND INTENTIONAL

Write your "What's Important Now" sheets. Develop a list of specific actions to take in the next three months to translate your inspiration related to calling into action. Give yourself momentum toward a future about which Jesus can say to you, "Well done, good and faithful servant." It starts now and it starts with being specific and intentional.

Final Words

Calling is something God does. It's something we respond to. And it draws us into a story and a beauty beyond our ability to imagine. The mystery is that we get to play a part in our own becoming. We participate actively in our discovery of calling!

God calls us all—so say yes and keep saying yes. Live your part. Step into your destiny and experience life to its fullest measure.

You'll never, ever regret it.

Visit www.personalcalling.org for supplemental resources.

Epilogue

by Bob Buford, Author of *Halftime*

I wrote the book *Finishing Well* to tell the stories of leaders compelled by their faith to accomplish great things. Even as I've traveled through this stage in my own life, I am working to follow the unique "good work" created for me to walk in, with a burden to be the best possible steward of what God has uniquely given me.

In researching *Finishing Well*, I found that the sweet spot of calling is a powerful mechanism for impact. Most importantly, an impact that contributes to an eternal scorecard that is measured in units of transformed lives. For the leaders I wrote about, personal calling is a beacon and roadmap for action. It cries out daily as a reminder that the One who made us in our mother's womb has divine plans for our lives.

One of the greatest ways for us to honor our Creator is by discovering and engaging the unique gifts and purposes he has given each us. Everyone has an Ephesians 2:10 calling that is meant to be lived out.

As I look out on the foreseeable future, my work swirls around, helping people activate their latent capacity into active energy via the powerful mechanism of personal calling. Take a minute to imagine what our world might look like if the body of Christ was truly activated and engaged in joining God's work, in the way he designed.

Within each person is the seed of a movement. This seed is activated by faithfully surrendering our will to the One who made us and wholeheartedly seeking to discover and engage the unique calling God places inside each of us. Personal calling is a profoundly significant gift of grace extended to us that tragically goes untapped by most people.

For centuries our forefathers sat on the sidelines and allowed trained clergy to read Scripture in a language the common man couldn't understand. Martin Luther sparked a movement by putting God's Word into the hands of the laity. We are now in the midst of another great movement where the lines between trained clergy and laity are becoming blurred, and the object of this transformation is each one of us acting as ministers of the gospel—twenty-four hours a day, seven days a week. We are blurring the lines by living lives of active engagement in our calling rather than passively watching others join in God's work.

I've never been more encouraged that the body of Christ is up for the challenge placed before us. We are poised for a "release movement" where the body of Christ is mobilized on their Ephesians 2:10 callings to do good works in the world. There are plenty of movement makers among us that have the ability to make significant impact in our communities and around the world. You are one of those if you are reading this book.

Several years ago I committed time to studying the stories that Jesus taught. I was amazed to find that of his thirty parables, fifteen focused on grace and forgiveness via a relationship with the One who made us (we don't earn our salvation), and fifteen focused on the idea of expectations for results and performance as an overflow of that relationship (salvation results in amazing action).

We are called first to a restored relationship of being with our Creator as we receive his gift of grace. The result and overflow of that restored relationship produces good works and deeds as we put our unique gifts and talents to work.

God calls us to himself for an eternal relationship and sends us to others that they might receive his grace.

When this life passes and we stand before God to give an account of our lives, I'm convinced only two questions will matter. First, what did you do about who Jesus said he is? Did you surrender to his lordship and direction? Second, what did you do with what he gave you to work with? He equipped you with a unique calling, so what did you do with it? These two questions form the core of loving God and loving people. To leave these gifts inactivated as latent energy is to miss the life Jesus intends for us.

Look at the disciples that walked with Jesus—they were men who were driven by mission and faith as they literally gave away their lives to the spread of the gospel. And look to Jesus himself—while he had his alone time with his Father, he was pretty active. There was not a hint of latency in his life. Thank you, God, for the models you've given us, most of all through your Son.

My challenge to you is to take the principles and framework articulated in *More* and get off the sidelines. Get in the game that God designed for you before the beginning of the world. In many respects, what Todd Wilson has done in this book is very similar to what Peter Drucker did for me. Todd is asking the right questions and providing the right feedback that plays out as encouragement, permission, clarity, and accountability.

Start by putting one foot in front of the other, and don't be surprised if God places you in the middle of a movement. I can promise you this—you will not take part in a movement, or anything significant, until you take that first step.

Get in the game! Be the difference maker God designed you to be.

Acknowledgments

This book has been a labor of love, taking over five years to complete. The acknowledgments are the hardest thing I've written, as so many people have informed the content of *More* and provided much-needed encouragement to me.

My wife, Anna, my sons, Benjamin and Christopher, and my parents, Rose and Gordon Wilson, are the people in this world who most directly and profoundly bring the stories in *More* to life for me personally. Our families hold the magnifying glasses that help us see and discern the clues into our personal calling.

Eric Reiss (www.story.gs) is an incredibly competent and selfless collaborator who has richly contributed to this book. Looking back, I can't imagine writing this without him. We are blessed by Eric's use of his sweet spot in this project.

Ron Furgerson, Brett Andrews, and Troy McMahon have been vital in helping me see my calling through the lens of the local church. Without even knowing it, they've provided just the right encouragement at just the right time to help me take crazy steps of faith toward my personal calling.

Mentor and friend Bob Buford is a kindred spirit who asked one simple yet profound question at just the right time: "What would it look like to live 100 percent in the sweet spot of your calling?" Bob's passion for seeing men and women discover and engage their unique Ephesians 2:10 calling is embedded throughout the pages of this book.

Rick Warren and Dr. Robert Coleman have shaped my paradigm of personal calling and helped me see that Jesus' way of discipleship is inseparable from living out our unique personal calling.

Alan Hirsch and Matt Carter encouraged me to write this book during a season in my life when it was possibly one of the last things I'd choose to do.

Bobby Harrington and Dave Ferguson have been encouraging friends, wholeheartedly sold out to Jesus and his mission here on earth.

Os Guinness read an early version of the draft manuscript and was not afraid to give me the critical feedback needed to prompt a comprehensive rewrite.

Mark Sweeney provided his expertise in writing and publishing books, and his help in structuring the outline of *More*, positioning the book to bless a larger audience than I could have achieved on my own.

Finally, Terri Saliba and Bill Couchenour, the sacrificial leaders who competently run the day-to-day operations of Exponential (www.exponential.org), enabled me to invest the time and energy required to finish this book. Their lives are a testimony to God's unique handiwork.

Notes

CHAPTER 1: TRUSTING THE AUTHOR OF OUR STORY

1. Os Guinness, in a personal email exchange with the author.

CHAPTER 4: SURRENDERING THE LEADING ROLE

1. John Ortberg, "God's Call Waiting," Christianity Today. com, March 3, 2008, http://www.christianitytoday.com/le/topics/soul/calling/cln80303b.html.
2. Os Guinness, *The Call*, 4, 6.
3. Larry Alex Taunton, "Listening to Young Atheists: Lessons for a Stronger Christianity," *TheAtlantic.com*, June 6, 2013, http://www.theatlantic.com/national/archive/2013/06/listening-to-young-atheists-lessons-for-a-stronger-christianity/276584/.

CHAPTER 5: REDEFINING SUCCESS

1. Peter Drucker, *Management*, rev. ed. (New York: HarperBusiness, 2008), xxxi.

CHAPTER 8: DISCOVERING MY UNIQUE ROLE

1. Gordon T. Smith, *Courage and Calling: Embracing Your God-Given Potential* (Downers Grove, Ill.: InterVarsity, 1999, 2011), 9, 10.

2. Cotton Mather, *A Christian at His Calling: Two Brief Discourses. One Directing a Christian in His General Calling; Another Directing Him in His Personal Calling* (Boston: Green & Allen, 1701).

CHAPTER 12: CRAFTED BY GOD: MY UNIQUE IDENTITY

1. Kevin and Kay Brennfleck, *Live Your Calling: A Practical Guide to Finding and Fulfilling Your Mission in Life* (San Francisco: Jossey-Bass, 2004), 6.

Find Your Calling

Using the
BE-DO-GO framework
from *More*

Visit
www.personalcalling.org

Features of PersonalCalling.org include:

- FREE "Find Your Calling" getting started guide and assessment

- FREE "Find Your Calling" online course to supplement *More*

- FREE tools and templates to supplement and enhance the exercises in *More*

- FREE "Find Your Calling" podcast featuring interviews with national leaders

- FREE articles and blog posts on personal calling